ME160m

Special children?

Special children?

(A theology of childhood)

Eric Lane

Grace Publications Trust

GRACE PUBLICATIONS TRUST
139 Grosvenor Avenue
London N5 2NH
England

Managing Editors
J. P. Arthur, M.A.
H. J. Appleby

ISBN 0 946462 399

Distributed by
EVANGELICAL PRESS
12 Wooler Street
Darlington
Co. Durham DL1 1RQ
England

Bible quotations, unless otherwise indicated, are from The New
International Version © Hodder & Stoughton

Printed in Great Britain by The Bath Press, Avon

Cover: L. L. Evans

Contents

Introduction

I have always had problems and questions about how believers should think of their children and treat them from the spiritual standpoint. Even when I shared the view that they were 'in the covenant', I found it hard to relate this to the evangelical view that regeneration is universally needed without exception for acceptance with God. Then, when I discarded the Paedo-baptist view I had the opposite problem: were my children precisely the same as those of unbelievers? Were they in no way different? Should I treat them as if they were pagans?

I found these questions to be fairly general among those who reject the Paedo-baptist theology of children. We who take the Baptist position are very clear on what we don't believe about children, and why, but we have left a vacuum in our theology. What do we believe the Bible teaches about children, apart from the fact that we don't baptise them until they come to faith? Is that the sum total of our concept? If so it is not surprising if we are despised as negative in our approach. I have felt for some time that what we need are not more books disproving infant baptism and proving that of believers, but rather something on how we should view our children positively and work this out in practice.

I was glad therefore when it was suggested that I did some research into the matter, as it gave me an incentive to tackle these questions. My starting place has to be the Bible. But which part? For if one thing is clear it is that the two testaments approach the subject differently. For the two testaments are the story of two covenants, or more accurately of two administrations of the one covenant of grace first revealed to Abraham long before the old covenant was made. The old was anticipatory of the new and therefore temporary, whereas the new is final and permanent, for it fulfils what was promised to Abraham. This difference between the two parts of Scripture affects everything, not least the position of children. It is essential to clarify this difference first. Then, on that basis, we can look at the many questions that arise.

As we do so it will become increasingly clear that, far from being demoted by the change from the old to the new covenant, our children are in fact far more 'special' than were those of the Israelites. So much is this the case that there is no reason why we should choke even on applying the word 'holy' to them. The fact that it means something different to us from what it does to our Paedo-baptist friends is in no way embarrassing. Rather, it is glorious.

I have learned much from researching and writing this book. If the enthusiasm of new discoveries has driven me 'over the top' in any place I hope you will understand and perhaps find the newness infectious. No doubt some of the findings will need qualification with maturer reflection, but at least they should be given respectful consideration.

Above all I hope that parents struggling to gain their children's interest in the gospel in these days when so much is against this will find real inward encouragement to persevere, and maybe a little practical help too.

Section 1:
Children under the old and new covenants

Part I:
Children under the old covenant

If we are to understand what it meant to be or have a child in Old Testament times we must leave our modern western culture behind and enter a very different world. The questions which exercise **us** are such as: how can the sterile have children? Are all methods of fertility legitimate? How can those who don't want children avoid them? What methods of contraception are right? What about the unwanted child? Is abortion ever right?

For those who have wanted children there are other questions: how can we make them happy? How can we enjoy our parenthood? Should we punish their misbehaviour? How can we prevent child abuse? How can we educate them for life in this highly acquisitive and competitive world? If we are **Christians** we will want to know how we should teach them the faith, bring them to trust Christ as their Saviour, know when they have come to a living faith and train them for the Christian life. We shall be concerned about their relationship with the world: how to protect them from anti-Christian ideas which may be taught them at school and how to help them withstand the hostility of a non-Christian society as they grow up.

We will find very little in the Old Testament to help us in these matters. This is not just because they are modern questions, but because the Old Testament's whole approach to children is different. 'The Old Testament shows little awareness of the distinctive psychology of children ... The question of a child's relationship to God, his individual religious life, is not discussed'.[1] The Old Testament is dominated by the idea of the child as a member of the group rather than as an individual in his own right. Post-Renaissance thinking in the west is individualistic, whereas the oriental still

possesses the group-centred outlook which characterised the ancient Hebrew people.

This did not mean that Hebrew parents did not love their children
as individuals. Jacob's deep grief when he thought he had lost
Benjamin has all the marks of genuine affection.[2] When David
wanted to show how God loved his people so much that he was even
prepared to overlook their sins, he used the analogy of a father's love
for his children.[3] God himself endorsed this through Jeremiah:
'How gladly would I treat you like sons and give you a desirable
land, the most beautiful inheritance of any nation. I thought you
would call me "Father" and not turn away from following me'
(Jeremiah 3:19). If this was to have any meaning for Hebrew parents
it must indicate a tenderness on their part towards their children.
Hosea compares God's patience with Israel to a parent teaching a
child to walk, in words that all parents can echo: 'It was I who taught
Ephraim to walk, taking them by the arms' (Hos. 11:3-4).

Nor does it mean that children as children were any different
from today. They loved playing as ours do;[4] they needed care; they
tended to naughtiness. There are hints of all this in the Old Testament but they are in the background. What is more prominent is that
children were important for different reasons. Whether they were
delightful or delinquent was not the main issue, which was simply
that they were there. They were essential for what was called the
mishpachah, the family, clan, tribe or nation. Nor was this concern
for the group merely nationalistic; it was deeply religious; it was
because this 'group' was in a special relationship with God, a
covenant relationship.

A. THEIR PLACE

There were three main areas in which children born to Israelite
parents were important.

1. They were essential for the fulfilment of the Creation mandate

'Be fruitful and increase' (Gen. 1:28) was God's first command to
the human race. The Fall did not bring about the withdrawal of this.
Even though sin was going to be transmitted God did not intend the
human race to die out. He still wanted mankind to rule the earth, and
for this children were essential. After the Fall and while actually

pronouncing the curse, God told the woman, 'You will give birth to children' (Gen. 3:16). It was after hearing of the curse of pain in child-bearing, hardships in child rearing and ultimate death that 'Adam named his wife Eve because she would become mother of all living' (Gen. 3:20).

This did not mean that all they had to do to ensure the next generation would obey God was to pass on the mandate of procreation. This is proved by the character and behaviour of Adam and Eve's first-born. Adam and Eve had a high regard for Cain to whom they gave a name that means 'acquired', as Eve said, 'with the help of the Lord' (Gen. 4:1). He was seen as the gift of God and trained to follow Adam as a tiller of the ground. Abel was less highly regarded. His name means 'vanity' and he was given the lowlier job of minding the sheep, like David later. But special favours do not necessarily produce good behaviour, nor does neglect necessarily lead to bad behaviour, under the old covenant or the new. (The seventh Earl of Shaftesbury, who was responsible for many of the great social reforms of the nineteenth century, especially in the case of children, himself was neglected as a child.) Adam and Eve came to realise this and saw Seth as the replacement for Abel;[5] like Abel 'a son in his (Adam's) own likeness' (Gen. 5:3), that is, the likeness of his godliness. It was a century or so after Abel when 'men began to call on the name of the Lord' (Gen. 4:26). From this time there was a succession of godly patriarchs whose extreme longevity helped to sustain this revival of godliness. [6] By the time of Noah the godly were again reduced to one family and God knew that what had happened before would happen again;[7] yet even then he renewed the mandate.[8]

These commands given to Adam and Noah came down to Israel through Abraham and Moses when other nations had lost the knowledge of them. Israel therefore was under an obligation to fulfil them. They must have families, not just because it was natural, but because God required it. So they saw the arrival of children not merely as part of a natural process but as God's gift, which he might grant or withhold.[9] When children came the parents rejoiced not just at seeing a new life but in receiving a token of God's blessing. 'With the help of the Lord I have brought forth a child', Eve cried out when her first baby was born (Gen. 4:1). Jacob spoke of his large family as God's gift,[10] as did Joseph.[11] Hannah was denied a child for many years and the birth of Samuel was a specific answer to her prayer,[12] which was written into his very name: 'She named him Samuel saying, "Because I asked the Lord for him"'. Children were something to rejoice over before God: 'Sons are a heritage from the Lord, children are a reward from him' (Ps. 127:3). Even some of the names drew attention to this, especially those based on *Nathan* ('given'), such as *Jonathan*, *Nathaniah*, as well as Nathan itself.

This is why wives were seen above all else as the mothers of children. The childless wife felt a failure and suffered much grief and frustration. Sarah was very angry with Hagar who had succeeded where she herself had failed.[13] Rachel was desperate for children: 'Give me children, or I'll die!' she cried out to her husband (Gen. 30:2). Hannah wept, fasted and cried to God over her childlessness.[14] On the other hand, Leah, a joyful mother but unhappy wife, hoped to win her husband's love by giving him children, as the names by which she called them indicate. Her first son she called Reuben, literally 'See, a son', although the Hebrew word has a hint of 'he has seen my misery', which was what she herself said, adding, 'Surely my husband will love me now' (Gen. 29:32). All this we should see, not so much as a lack of fulfilment or a sense of personal failure but rather as a breach of the creation mandate of Genesis 1:28.

2. They were essential for the perpetuation of the family name

The people of the old covenant knew very little about life after death. What lay beyond the grave was darkness, which they called *sheol*, described so poignantly in Psalm 88:3-9. The dead do not praise God but 'go down to silence' (Ps. 115:17). Job looked forward to death simply as an end to his sufferings. He had no concept of conscious happiness, worship of God or fellowship with him, or even of his punishment. He would be as oblivious as a still-born child.[15]

Hopes of immortality and resurrection were very slow to develop and a subject of dispute among the authorities. There are occasional prophetic outbursts about a resurrection, such as Job's in 19:25-27, Isaiah's in 26:19 and Daniel's in 12:2, but how far they were comprehended by the speakers, let alone the hearers, is doubtful. A man's hope of living on after death lay chiefly with the children to whom he passed his name. 'The belief that a man lived on in those who came after him was far more than a figure of speech ... The value of the "name" to Hebrew thinking was that it embodied something of the life of the individual whose name it was. The whole of a man's personality was summed up in his name. Where a man's name lived on there he lived on too'.[16] The desperate measures resorted to by the daughters of Lot show how deep this desire went — it proved stronger than natural decency.[17]

This was no mere personal hang-up but given divine sanction in the law of 'levirate' marriage. A childless widow was to be married to the brother of her dead husband, provided he was single, 'so that his name will not be blotted out from Israel' (Deut. 25:5-6). This at least partly explains the marriage of Boaz and Ruth (see Ruth 4). It was this concern that motivated the daughters of Zelophehad to petition for land, not for themselves but lest 'our father's name disappear from his clan because he has no son' (Num. 27:1-4). This led to a new law to cover a situation where a man died without a son — his inheritance must be kept in the family.[18] It also gave substance to the plea of the woman of Tekoa on behalf of David's son Absalom. [19]

The worst thing that could befall a man was the loss of his children. When God really wanted to strike terror into hearts he used this threat: 'Prepare a place to slaughter his sons for the sins of their forefathers: they are not to rise to inherit the land and cover the earth with their cities' (Isa. 14:21). The way to destroy a nation was to destroy her children rather than her army: 'I will rise against them, declares the Lord Almighty. I will cut off from Babylon her name and survivors, her offspring and descendants, declares the Lord' (Isa. 14:22). Israel herself was in danger of this at the hands of the Pharaohs Amenhotep I and Thutmose I in Exodus 1:15-22. This danger recurred seven centuries later when their apostasy provoked God to raise up the Assyrians against them: 'The people of Samaria must bear their guilt, because they have rebelled against their God. They will fall by the sword; **their little ones will be dashed to the ground, their pregnant women ripped open'** (Hos. 13:16).

This explains the dreadful command of *herem*, 'devoting to destruction', when in war it was not only the soldiers who were to be slain but all men along with their wives and children.[20] It also explains the horrendous words of Psalm 137:8-9: 'O daughter of Babylon, doomed to destruction, happy is he who repays you for what you have done to us — he who seizes your infants and dashes them against the rocks.' This was not vindictiveness of a particularly cruel kind, but genocide as a judgement on Babylon from God himself in fulfilment of his threat in the words of Isaiah quoted above.

It is also the reason why male children were preferred to female. This has nothing to do with chauvinism in the modern sense but with the need to perpetuate the family name. Daughters who married would take the name of the family they married into. Only a son would keep his father's name alive. So Hannah prayed specifically for a son.[21] The beautiful wedding songs of Solomon (Ps. 127,128) glory in the gift of sons who are 'a heritage from the Lord ... a reward from him ... Like arrows in the hand of a warrior are sons born in one's youth'. The birth of a son was celebrated as the event which saved the family name.

3. They were essential for the continuance of the covenant with God

In Israel children were the gift not just of providence but of grace. The people of Israel were in a special relationship with God because they were children of Abraham whom he took into covenant relationship with himself, saying 'I will ... be your God and the God of your descendants after you' (Gen. 17:7). This set them apart from all nations on the face of the earth. In order to make it viable he gave them their own land and pledged it to them in perpetuity. The covenant promise was encapsulated in the rite of circumcision: 'This is my covenant with you and your descendants after you ... Every male among you shall be circumcised' (Gen. 17:9-14). It branded the covenant in the flesh of the new-born son, in his organ of reproduction. It signified that he was entering this relationship and that he would eventually bequeath it to his own children.

The only qualification for the covenant of circumcision was birth to Israelite parents: 'The male was regarded as a member of the covenant community by virtue of his birth'.[22] To be uncircumcised was to be outside the covenant; it was the heathen who were uncircumcised. Any Israelite who failed in this respect was a covenant-breaker and could be 'cut off from his people' (Gen. 17:14), that is, put to death. This was why God threatened Moses with death if he failed to circumcise his son before returning to the people.[23]

The importance of children was further emphasised by the consecration of the first-born to God, which he required from the time of the first Passover.[24] These represented the whole nation and this responsibility was balanced by the first-born's right to a double portion of the father's estate.[25] This highlighted the privilege of a nation which God called his 'son' (Hos. 11:1) and of which he was 'Father' (Deut. 32:6).

To have children, especially sons, was therefore vital to the Israelite, not only to fulfil the creation mandate and perpetuate his family name but above all to continue the covenant relationship between God and his people. Abraham himself had realised this even before the formal making of the covenant.[26] Abraham is the prototype Israelite father. The birth of Isaac meant more to him than the birth of a son does to any of us [27] and similarly the threatened loss of him in chapter 22 was a double test — both of his natural affection and his faith in the covenant-making God.

When Isaac became a man Abraham went to great lengths to ensure that the covenant would continue in his line by seeking out a relative to be his wife. He made his servant solemnly 'swear by the Lord the God of heaven and the God of earth that you will not get a wife for my son from the daughters of the Canaanites ... but will go to my country and my own relatives and get a wife for my son Isaac' (Gen. 24:3-4). The words with which Rebekah's family blessed her on her marriage are prophetic: 'Our sister, may you increase to thousands upon thousands; may your offspring possess the gates of their enemies' (Gen. 24:60). They are the language in which God called Abraham.[28] This procedure was repeated when Isaac's son Jacob came to marriageable age.[29] Jacob's daughter Dinah was preserved from marrying outside the family in a drastic way. When she had slept with the Hivite prince of Shechem and general intermarriage between them and Jacob's family was being negotiated, Simeon and Levi came and slaughtered every male in Shechem.[30] By the time of his flight to Egypt Jacob had established a numerous family[31] and had thus secured the continuance of the covenant in Abraham's line for generations to come.

This was why, when Israelites had children, they rejoiced, not just because the human race would continue and their names endure but because God's covenant would go on. Child-bearing thus became listed as one of the promised blessings attached to the covenant which God renewed as the people entered the land: 'If you fully obey the Lord your God all these blessings will come upon you ... You will be blessed in the city and blessed in the country. **The fruit of your womb will be blessed'** (Deut. 28:1-4).

B. THEIR EDUCATION

It was these principles, especially the last, that governed the way in which Hebrew children were educated. Education meant something very different to them from what it means to us. They had no theories of education and no specialist training designed to prepare children for life in the world, for they lived, not in the world, but in a **theocracy.** They were under the direct rule of God, who was not only the One they worshipped but their 'judge ... lawgiver and king' (Isa. 33:22). Their concern was not so much for the welfare of the individual child as for the covenant relation of the whole nation with God. Their eyes were not on academic success or securing the best jobs with the highest salaries. Nor did they have the problem of countering secularism in education that Christians face today. They simply wanted to bring up children who would receive the teaching they themselves had been given, so that in due course they would pass it on to their children, that is, the knowledge of God, his covenant and laws.

1. The educators

It was for this reason that education was entrusted to parents who had received it from their own fathers. Solomon sought to pass on to his children what David had taught him.[32] There was no special-ised teaching or knowledge until after the Exile, when the Rabbinic and synagogue system developed. The sons of kings might have had tutors, as Ahab's children did,[33] but this did not become general until the Roman Empire.[34] There were no schools until about 100 B.C., set up by Simeon ben Shelach. Josephus refers to Herod 'going to school' as a child.[35]

What was important was that children should be instructed in the acts and laws of God: what he had done and what he demanded. The things that had been seen and heard at Sinai must be passed on down the generations.[36] The demands God had imposed on that first generation were to be repeated to the next and to each succeeding generation.[37] Education did not progress with the advance of knowl-edge, learning and technology, as ours does. It centred on what was basic and once-for-all: the events surrounding the foundation of the theocratic nation. This continued unchanged down the generations and centuries. The pattern began with Abraham, who was admitted to the secret purposes of God because he was also entrusted with passing them on.[38]

The education process began with circumcision, for this confirmed that the child was in the covenant. It meant no more than this and said nothing about the spiritual state of the child, actual or potential. Not all circumcised people were spiritually alive. Ishmael was circumcised although he was denied the blessings of the covenant given to Isaac.[39] Even aliens who lived among them were circumcised.[40] In these cases no doubt it was done to give them a certain sense of security of tenure in the land they were to share with Isaac's descendants. The doctrine of the remnant of later times shows that in fact only a minority was truly spiritual. But this in no way affected the upbringing and education of the child.

At first it seems the mother was more prominent and that the care of the infant child was left to her. 'Do what seems best to you', was Elkanah's comment when Hannah consulted him about Samuel (1 Sam. 1:23). The mother might even decide on the child's name, as both Leah and Hannah did.[41] Female servants also played a part[42] as did grandmothers.[43] As the child grew big enough to share in household duties, so the father gradually took over the training. 'In ancient Hebrew society trades would normally have been hereditary and the child, particularly the boy, would at an early age have been set to work with his father and thus learned from him'.[44]

So it is the father who is to 'command his children' (Gen. 18:17-19), to warn them, as so much of Proverbs does, and to 'make known' or 'declare the ways of God to them' (Exod. 18:20). This education was not done in formal classes at set times but in the ordinary course of domestic and business life: 'when you sit at home and when you walk along the road ... ' (Deut. 6:6f; 11:19). It was in the home as well as at the national shrine that God was worshipped and his feast celebrated. The Passover was a particular opportunity for instruction because it aroused the child's curiosity and provoked questions which would enable more instruction to be given.[45] They were also to keep before their children the awesome way in which the covenant was originally made at Sinai.[46]

Gradually the child's interest in the things of God generally would be aroused and he would make more enquiries.[47] Families attended public worship together[48] so that children were present at the public reading of the Law every seven years.[49] But all this did not mean the mother dropped out of the education process. In Proverbs she is coupled with the father in the moral instruction of the child so prominent in that book.[50] The instruction of King Lemuel by his mother, although probably emanating from Egypt, is included in this great educational manual for the covenant people.[51] It would be in these ways that the child, like Samuel, would 'grow' (1 Sam. 2:26).

To have children and teach them the facts about their God was not enough. They must be taught to **obey** his laws, beginning with the duty of respect for and submission to their parents, as the fifth commandment required: 'Honour your father and your mother, so that you may live long in the land the Lord your God is giving you' (Exod. 20:12). The promise included there is the covenant itself: the enjoyment of God's favour in the land he had given his people, where they could live separate from the non-covenant nations. It is significant that this promise is attached to this commandment rather than to any of the others. It shows that the continuance of the covenant relationship depended absolutely on the way children were brought up. So the promise of a long and happy life in the land is not to be seen as made to the individual child as such, but to the whole nation. 'The incentive and motive of obedience is the promise not so much of individual longevity as of the survival and triumph of the whole people in the promised land. It follows that insubordination in children is a threat to the whole community of God's people'.[52] If the children failed the whole covenant would fail, but if they were faithful like their parents, the covenant would continue.

The reason for this stringency lay in the peculiar relationship between the father and the rest of his family. He was the Ba'al, the Lord, a name afforded not only to foreign deities but to God himself.[53] The Israelite father was to his children what God was to him. He 'owned' his children as much as he did his land and cattle. [54] He might sell them into slavery,[55] though not to a foreigner;[56] they might be seized by his creditors in lieu of repayment[57] or even offered as hostages.[58] The father who failed to maintain discipline over his children was held responsible for their behaviour and thus shared in their punishment. Eli's sons were guilty of bringing the worship of God into disrepute. Eli merely rebuked them, with the result that God sent a prophet to lay the blame on Eli's shoulders, predict the death of the miscreant sons and the removal of the priesthood from Eli's family. It was this prophecy that God confirmed to Samuel when he spoke to him for the first time (1 Sam.

2:12—3:18). Later, David was to suffer for his leniency with his sons. Because he took no action against Amnon for the rape of Tamar, Absalom took the law into his own hands and murdered Amnon. Because he failed to punish Absalom for murder, that young man was left free to usurp David's throne. It is not surprising that lawlessness abounded during David's reign, as he himself complained.[59] The inspired record in 1 Kings 1:6 attributes the troublesome ambition and precocity of Adonijah to his father David's failure to discipline him.

So absolute was the requirement of obedience that a son who refused it could be charged, tried, condemned and stoned to death.[60] This severe rule was given to a nation which was strictly forbidden to do what other nations did — sacrifice their children to appease the wrath of their gods.[61] The execution of a Hebrew son was never sacrificial but always judicial. Their crime was not just the dishonouring of parents, nor ingratitude and contempt for those who had brought them into the world and nourished them (death would have been an excessive punishment for such a crime) but that such behaviour threatened the survival of the whole nation. Children who disobeyed their parents were disobeying God, for it was he who required this obedience. Under the old covenant God's method was to continue his favour through physical generation, not spiritual regeneration.[62] If children did not follow in their parents' footsteps in relation to God, the covenant with Israel could not endure.

2. The education

As regards the **process of education** the Book of Proverbs gives us the most detailed information. It was a kind of education manual, showing how the 'wisdom' of God could be transmitted to the rising generation. If it is Solomon instructing his sons as his father had instructed him, as 4:1-4 suggests, then he is giving an example to all the people. While Proverbs is packed with 'worldly wisdom' or universal common sense, it is also seen as part of godliness: 'The fear of the Lord is the beginning of knowledge' (1:7). It is a book of discipline and education for Hebrew households. The following points are of most relevance to us:

a. Its estimate of the child's condition

Proverbs explains something of why the child needs this discipline. He is naturally 'foolish' (22:15), not in the sense of unintelligent, but that he is inclined to triviality, sloth and rebelliousness. Parental discipline 'will drive it far from him' (22:15). Proverbs does not develop the theology of fallen human nature in the way the New Testament does. Indeed this is true of the Old Testament generally. It contains the only record of the events of the Fall in Genesis 3, and it frequently exposes the corruption of human nature.[63] But it rarely if ever explains the latter by the former. It is Paul who expounds the idea of 'imputed guilt' and explains that it is this that has poisoned human nature morally and spiritually.[64] We have to take this into account in studying what Proverbs teaches about the upbringing of children, for which they relied almost totally on discipline rather than theology. We would combine discipline with teaching the new birth, which truly 'drives out' the principle of disobedience within our children's natures.

In fact under the old covenant the child was not regarded as morally responsible: he does not know the difference between good and evil.[65] The child is the 'simple' one of Proverbs 1:4, ignorant of what God requires and what constitutes character; also of how to relate to other people. He needs to be taught 'discernment' in order to make right choices, which will lead to right actions. This does not however exempt him from divine judgement, for this may fall on the children for the sins of their fathers.[66] God may treat the whole nation 'as one man' (Num. 14:12,15). He may on the other hand spare the children, not because they are innocent, but rather to demonstrate his mercy, as he did when he kept the young from falling in the Sinai desert and allowed them to enter the land.[67]

This natural foolishness was changed, not as it is under the gospel by the new birth, but by 'the rod of discipline' (Prov. 22:15). To impose this was absolutely vital because of the extreme penalties a child would suffer if he grew up to bring shame and grief on his parents by his behaviour.[68] He may actually suffer the death penalty: 'Do not withhold discipline from a child; if you punish him with the rod **he will not die**. Punish him with the rod and **save his soul from death**' (Prov. 23:13f). The word for 'death' there is *sheol*, 'the grave', which refers here to an untimely death as a criminal, as compared with *gehenna*, 'hell', everlasting punishment, from which only salvation delivers. It is in view of such a prospect that a parent is to chasten his son: 'Discipline your son, for in that there is hope; do not be a willing party to his death' (Prov. 19:18).

b. *Its advice about the company the child should seek or avoid*

He must not, for example, get involved with muggers or highwaymen because of the severe penalties attached to those crimes.[69] He must beware of promiscuous women and prostitutes, a subject to which much space is devoted in Proverbs.[70] No doubt it was very easy to be tempted into such relationships, but very difficult to disentangle oneself without dire trouble, as those passages show. Children were to be home lovers and to please their parents rather than indulge their lusts.

The dangers of being enticed into street crime through associating with criminals, villains and the immoral were much greater for Hebrew children even than they are for ours, great as these are. The death penalty was widely applied, and for a family to lose its son in these circumstances was to lose the blessings which these children were given by God to preserve: the perpetuation of the race, the family name and the covenant with God.

c. *The motive it appeals to in encouraging discipline*

This is not infrequently the happiness of the parents themselves, which is in fact the theme of the first real proverb: 'A wise son brings joy to his father, but a foolish son grief to his mother'.[71] This does not mean that the parents were essentially selfish and had no 'better nature' to appeal to. It was rather that they, especially the father, were God's representatives and their happiness was bound up with God's. Therefore the parents' chastening of the child was also God's.[72] A happy relationship with his people, in which God could delight, depended on the way each generation behaved toward him and his laws. It was not just that well-behaved children meant a peaceful household in which children were helpful and brought their parents no disgrace, but that such households attracted the blessing of God. God's chief delight lay in his people and would only exist if they acknowledged and obeyed him. A fresh generation could not assume he would automatically continue his favours. They must keep the covenant as their fathers had. The responsibility for this was laid very much on the parents. So when we read that 'a wise son brings joy to his father', we are to see this, not as a mere observation on human life, but a profound theological statement. The wisdom to be instilled into a child was not only about acceptable behaviour but godly living.[73] A parent who achieves this has served his nation and done his part in maintaining the covenant.

This discipline was not confined to childhood but must continue through life. So long as parents live their children must respect them: 'Train a child in the way he should go, and when he is old he will not turn from it' (22:6). This would serve as an example to their own children as they sought to teach them respect for themselves. If a grown-up son who becomes a parent goes on honouring his father, his children are more likely to honour both father and grandfather.[74] Old Testament society was not, like ours, about happy families, but something more serious — preserving the covenant relationship with God until the arrival of the Mediator of the new covenant. The question that arises is: when he did come, how would it affect the matter of parents and children?

References

Section 1, Part 1

1   J.S. Pridmore: *The New Testament Theology of Childhood*, p.1.
2   Gen. 42:36
3   Ps. 103:13
4   Zech. 8:5

Section 1, Part 1, A

5   Gen. 4:25
6   Gen. 5:4-32
7   Gen. 8:21
8   Gen. 9:1
9   Gen. 16:1f; 17:6, 15f; 20:17f
10 Gen. 33:5
11 Gen. 48:9
12 1 Sam. 1:11-17
13 Gen. 16:1-6
14 1 Sam. 1:8-11
15 Job 3:11-19
16 Pridmore, op. cit. pp. 5-6
17 Gen. 19:30-38
18 Num. 27:8-11
19 2 Sam. 14:1-7
20 e.g. Deut. 20:16-18
21 1 Sam. 1:11
22 D. Kingdon: *Children of Abraham*, p.69
23 Exod. 4:24-26
24 Exod. 13:2
25 Deut. 21:16f
26 Gen. 15:1-3
27 Gen. 21:1-7
28 Gen. 12:3; 13:6
29 Gen. 28:1-5
30 Gen. 34
31 Gen. 46

Section 1, Part 1, B

32 Prov. 4:1-4
33 2 Kings 10:1-5
34 Gal. 3:24f; 4:1f
35 Antiquities 15.x.5.
36 Deut. 4:9f
37 Deut. 4:40; 6:6
38 Gen. 18:17-19
39 Gen. 17:20f
40 Gen. 17:23-27
41 see also 1 Chr. 4:9; 7:16
42 Gen. 24:59; 2 Kings 11:1-3
43 Ruth 4:10
44 Pridmore, op. cit. p.22
45 Exod. 12:26f
46 Deut. 4:9-14
47 Deut. 6:20-25; Josh. 4:21
48 Deut. 12:7; Joel 2:16
49 Deut. 31:10-13
50 Prov. 1:8; 6:20
51 Prov. 31:1-9
52 Pridmore, op. cit. p.28
53 e.g. Isa. 54:5 (Heb.)
54 Deut. 7:13; 28:4
55 Exod. 21:7
56 Neh. 5:5
57 2 Kings 4:1; Isa. 50:1
58 Gen. 42:37
59 e.g. Ps. 94
60 Exod. 21:15,17; Deut. 21:18-21
61 Lev. 20:1-5; Deut. 12:29-31
62 Ps. 103:17f; 112:1f
63 Gen. 6:5; 8:21; Ps. 51:7; 58:3; Jer. 17:9
64 see Rom. 5
65 Deut. 1:39; Isa. 7:15f
66 Exod. 20:5
67 Num. 14:31
68 Prov. 29:15
69 Prov. 1:10-19
70 Prov. 2:16-19; ch. 5; 6:20—7:27
71 Prov. 10:1, see also 15:20; 17:21; 29:3, 15, 17
72 Prov. 3:11f
73 Prov. 1:7
74 Prov. 17:6

Part II:
Children under the new covenant

What effect did the coming of the promised Redeemer have on the Bible's theology of children? How does their status under the new covenant differ from that under the old? We may look at this from the standpoint of the two areas investigated in Part 1: their **place** and their **education**.

A. THEIR PLACE

1. The importance of the child

We have had people from certain other cultures among us long enough to observe a difference between their approach to family life and ours. Their families tend to be larger: they have on average more children; their households often comprise three generations; they prefer the discomfort and inconvenience of crowding into a few rooms to the separation of the generations which would result from having more space. Some arrange marriages for their children and implement these at an early age, which can bring a fourth generation and extra bodies into the household.

Our way is to approach family life from an economic standpoint. We tend to marry only when there is a prospect of living apart from parents. We only have them under our roof when age, illness or poverty compel it. We delay having children until we can manage comfortably on one salary. We regulate the number of our children by the size of our home and income.

Sometimes this care is taken because we don't want to have to make sacrifices for the sake of having children, or at least to minimise those sacrifices. But there is usually a higher motive — we want to be able to give them the best possible help: to feed and clothe them well, give them space to live, as much educational help and enjoyable leisure as possible; and above all the maximum attention from us.

However, many have a sneaking envy for the other culture. While our family relationships tend to break down and our families to break up, theirs seem to stick together. While our children get out of control theirs seem to have a discipline which keeps them out of trouble and produces polite and well-behaved children, well on the way to becoming responsible adults. We wonder therefore if our approach to family life is the best one, why there is this difference and how it originated.

The answer is that it comes from the influence of Christianity on our culture. Christianity stresses the individual rather than the group. Not only is this one of the basic differences between the western and oriental approach, but it is also what distinguishes the new covenant view of childhood from that of the old. As we have seen, the Old Testament is dominated by the idea of the child as a member of the group rather than as an individual in his own right. The child was essential for the *mishpachah* — the family, clan or nation. This concept still characterises Judaism as it does oriental society.

The reason we in the west have departed from it is that the coming of the gospel brought about a change. This change was initiated by Jesus himself in his earthly ministry. When asked, 'Who is the greatest in the kingdom of heaven?' he 'called a little child and had him stand among them' (Matt. 18:1f). The question was about 'the kingdom of heaven' — this new society Jesus was founding under himself. It was to replace the kingdom of Israel because it was to be as wide as the world itself, comprehending all nations. The old covenant, in which one nation alone constituted the people of God, was giving way to a new covenant in which the people of God would be drawn from all nations. The promise made to Abraham was in process of fulfilment: 'in you all nations of the earth will be blessed' (Gen. 12:3).

In this new society 'the great' are individual believers, even a child. The child was no longer a means to an end — the preservation of the nation — but a member of the kingdom in his own right. One little child believing in him qualified for the term 'great' in his kingdom. In fact anyone of any age who in simplicity believed on him was in the same position (Matt. 18:3f). But the child is the model believer — that is, the child as an individual not as a genus. Jesus uses phrases like 'whoever humbles himself **like this child**' and 'whoever welcomes **a little child**' (v.5) and 'if anyone causes **one of these little ones** ... to sin' (v.6).

This approach to children was quite revolutionary. Everywhere in the ancient world children, along with women, old men and slaves, were viewed as physically weak burdens on society with little value in the community. In Greece and Rome it was an accepted practice to abandon unwanted children along the roadside to die. It was new in other ways too, even to the Jews. Jewish rabbis never singled out little children as Jesus did. Even less did they make great theological statements about their importance. Jesus went as far as to say that the judgement of hell would fall on someone just for leading one little child into sin (Matt. 18:6-9). Even his disciples could not take this on board, for when a little later people began to bring their children to him so that he could lay his hands on them, they rebuked them (Matt. 19:13). But Jesus rebuked the disciples and received the children.

To go back to Matthew 18, Jesus developed his teaching on children by speaking of how God includes them in the ministry of his angels (v.10). This led him to tell the parable of the one lost sheep — something in itself quite new since it showed that God cares about one lost sinner as much as a whole group. On this occasion he connected it with his teaching on children, since he concludes by saying, 'In the same way your Father in heaven is not willing that **any of these little ones** should be lost' (v.14).

There is no question that the individualistic approach that characterises western society is the heritage of the teaching of Christ. The lost sheep was important for itself. So is every sinner, including even a single child. No longer is he there to perpetuate his clan or nation but is important for himself.

Why then does our individualistic approach seem to work less well than the oriental group approach? Why does it seem to produce disintegration and delinquency? This is not because of the individualism itself, but because, in the hand of sinners it is, like everything else, open to abuse. It is often said that the fragmentation of the Protestant Church is due to the doctrines of justification by faith and the priesthood of all believers. This does not make the doctrine wrong, only the way it is handled. In the same way the rationalist and materialist attitudes to life (which we associate with 'the Enlightenment') are the grandchildren of the Reformation concept of the right of private enquiry. This does not make the Reformation wrong; it only shows how sinful men abuse the best gifts of God.

In the same way the teaching of Christ that the individual is important in himself is the basis of our personal salvation. It applies equally to children as to adults. But such teaching is open to abuse like everything else. It was not long before the gospel of free forgiveness through faith only was being made an excuse for 'continuing in sin'.[1] Is it surprising that the same should happen with every other teaching of the new covenant? Moreover, the oriental way itself is far from perfect. The cohesion of the family has a cost — not only the early arranged marriage but the whole atmosphere of submission, fear and bondage. This has become a defence mechanism which resists the offer of the gospel to members of the family.

The other New Testament writers say little about children. They mainly addressed themselves to churches and wrote about issues which cropped up and had to be dealt with immediately. They are not treatises thought out at leisure which cover the whole body of Christian truth. However, in two of his letters Paul did address himself to the children in the congregation. In Ephesians 5:21 — 6:9 he was writing of the need for mutual submission in all relationships. In the course of this he spoke directly to the children in 6:1 and added a caveat to the fathers warning them against discouraging their children in verse 4. There is a similar passage in Colossians 3:20-21. Paul would know that his letters were communicated to a whole congregation probably by an elder reading them out at a gathering of the church. When the subject lent itself to so doing he spoke to the children present about how the point under discussion applied to them. They were important and therefore included!

2. The child as a token of God's blessing

Under the old covenant the supreme blessing was to be the people of God in a way no other nation was. But the fruits of this were mainly material gifts, as is seen in the blessing of Jacob in Genesis 49 and the blessings of Moses in Deuteronomy 28 and 33. Chief among these was the gift of children. Only as God gave them children could Israel fulfil the creation mandate to 'multiply' and ensure the continuance of the covenant between God and his people. So the birth of children, particularly sons, was the occasion of great rejoicing.[2] On the other hand, to be denied children was a reproach, as the grief of Sarah, Rachel and Hannah all show.[3] The childless woman felt she had failed not only her husband but the whole nation, indeed God himself.

When we come to the gospel age we find a different concept of God's blessing. Jesus made it clear from the start that the blessings of God through him were spiritual, as his 'Beatitudes' make clear.[4] Nowhere does he speak of material gifts as tokens of God's approval, in fact he even pronounced the poor and afflicted blessed. [5] To be reproached and even persecuted now was a blessing![6] The concept of 'blessing' is developed by the apostles in their account of salvation in Christ.[7] 'Blessing' is about what God has done for us in his Son: chosen, justified, sanctified and glorified us.

As for children, no longer is the childless woman to regard herself or be regarded as under a divine curse for which she must blame herself or be despised by society. Indeed to have children now can be a source of sorrow where they do not share their parents' faith.[8] Of course the bonds of natural affection are still as strong as ever and have the approval and sympathy of Jesus, as his healings of children in answer to the frantic appeals of their parents indicate. [9] He even compared the joy of child-bearing to that of seeing him risen from the dead.[10]

But, no longer are children essential to a person's assurance of God's favour as they had been under the old covenant. Indeed no longer is it necessary even to be married to have an honourable place in the kingdom of Christ. When Jesus raised the standard of marriage to preclude divorce except in the case of unfaithfulness, the disciples wondered whether singleness was not the lesser evil. [11] The current view of the single state did not make it an attractive option! Jesus however did not go along with this view. He didn't say, 'Don't go to the other extreme — marriage isn't **that** bad!' Rather he **recommended** the single state as a special calling.[12] Indeed he actually referred to it as a 'gift' — of God, that is. In the new economy not only are children a gift and token of God's blessing, but so is the lack of them, even of a spouse!

But Jesus did not go to the other extreme of elevating chastity above marriage. There is a calling to marry and have children, and a calling to remain single 'because of the kingdom of heaven'. This might be for a physical reason, such as a disability or non-heterosexual orientation. It might be because of a dearth of potential partners of like faith. It might be because of some service which would make it unfair on a wife or children to involve them. This seems to be how the apostle Paul viewed his own position. He comes over to us as either a bachelor or widower and glories in the freedom it gives him to preach the gospel anywhere.[13] But he is far from deprecating marriage.[14] Both conditions are for those called to them.[15]

So, while children always have been and always will be the gift and blessing of God, they no longer have that place above childlessness that they occupied under the old covenant. God has even greater blessings for believers in Christ!

3. The child and the family name

To us the people of Israel seem unduly obsessed with the idea of perpetuating their names. We might compare them with the aristocrat's agonising over the dying out of his ancient line, or even with a king's desperation to continue his dynasty. So important was the family name in Israel that they valued sons far above daughters because the latter would only change their names on marrying. But, unlike our royals or nobles, they had divine sanction for this. So-called 'levirate' marriage was written into the law.[16] A man **must** marry his brother's widow if he is free to, 'so that his name will not be blotted out from Israel'. As was seen in the previous section, what lay behind this had much to do with the uncertainty as to what lay beyond death. Did a man live on? If so, in what state? They had very little idea and took refuge in the hope of living on in their children who would bear their name and keep their memory alive. Retaining their land in the family would help this process and ensure the continuation of the family name.

The New Testament has very little interest in names. After establishing that Jesus could be proved to be of the line of David on both his natural mother's and his legal father's side, the New Testament loses interest in genealogies. Paul, who had once been proud of his ancestry, equates the discussion of the subject along with myths and false doctrines![17] The people of God no longer make it their chief aim in life to have a family, especially of sons. Their great desire is to obtain a place in Christ's eternal kingdom, for themselves, their dependants and anyone else. Paul was one who had gloried in the purity of his Jewish blood until he came to know Christ. From that time his aim was to know him increasingly, even though it meant suffering. Ultimately he wanted to die like him and be raised again.[18]

This change of attitude was due to the light shed on the hereafter by Jesus and the gospel. Believers have 'a living hope through the resurrection of Christ from the dead' that they will 'enter into an inheritance that can never perish, spoil or fade' (1 Pet. 1:3f). Paul was full of this hope: 'to die is gain ... I desire to depart and be with Christ which is better by far' (Phil. 1:21-23). This is what he preached everywhere, making eschatology part of his gospel, not a special subject for advanced Christians. It was part of the message he preached during his brief stay in Thessalonica.[19]

Those who have this hope do not need to live to have children above all else. If God gives them a wife or husband they are glad. If he gives a couple children they thank him. While they would like a mixed family, they do not give way to grief if they only have daughters. While they are happy if they have sons, and if these sons also have sons, their happiness and sense of fulfilment are not dependent on this. God has given them a better hope. They themselves are immortal, which a family name can never be.

4. The child and the covenant

There was a far higher motive for Israelites to have children than the continuation of their name or even the assurance of God's favour. This was the covenant between God and them. God had taken Abraham into this special relationship with himself and extended it to his descendants through Isaac. This was why the prospect of a son dominated the minds of Abraham and Sarah for the first twenty-five years of their pilgrimage. Isaac was the key to the fulfilment of the promise to make a new and 'great nation' out of Abraham. No one else could belong to this nation other than his descendants. To seal this promise God gave a sign — a mark in the flesh, circumcision. This was his way of closing the deal and securing Abraham's acceptance of the privilege of being God's covenant people. So the conditions necessary to enjoying this special relationship with God were birth of a descendant of Isaac and circumcision. All others were outside the covenant.

How vital it was therefore for Israelites to have children! There was no other way by which God's covenant people could continue. And it must be through sons, for they alone could receive the sign of the covenant, circumcision, in their reproductive organ. So this was what above all made the birth of sons to Israelite families such an occasion of rejoicing. The 'Wedding Song' (Ps. 45) mounts up to this climax: 'Your sons will take the place of your fathers; you will make them princes throughout the land. I will perpetuate your memory through all generations; therefore the nations will praise you for ever' (vv. 16f).

When we come to the new covenant we find both continuity and discontinuity. Jeremiah had indicated the continuity in his prophecy that under the new as under the old covenant 'I will be your God and you will be my people' (Jer. 31:33b). God's covenant of grace has been and always will be a relationship with him, even at the end of the world.[20] But Jeremiah also indicates a change coming in the way the covenant would be administered. He speaks of laws written on the heart and a direct knowledge of God.[21] Ezekiel develops this by speaking of the sprinkling of water on the unclean and the gift of a new heart and spirit.[22] Jesus announced to Nicodemus that this was now being fulfilled: 'except a man is born of water and the Spirit he cannot enter the kingdom of God' (John 3:5). The new birth is the fulfilment of Ezekiel's prophecy of cleansing and renewal. No longer does a person enter into covenant relationship with God by being born of a circumcised father, a son of Abraham. He must be 'born of God' himself. He must receive not circumcision but Christ, and he will be 'born of God ... called a son of God' (John 1:12f).

This means that having children is no longer essential to maintaining a covenant people on earth. Indeed the New Testament says very little about 'covenant' but much about 'kingdom' — not a national but a divine kingdom ('the kingdom of God'), not a political but a spiritual kingdom ('the kingdom of heaven'). In keeping with this, the need is to be 'born of God', 'born from above' or 'born of the Spirit'. The way into this kingdom is taken out of the hands of man and performed entirely by the persons of the Godhead: the Father to plan and call, the Son to mediate and the Spirit to regenerate.

God has no longer tied himself to making the children of those already his people into covenant children. He frequently does so but not invariably. On the other hand he often goes to other families and

calls someone born of parents outside the covenant. God is entirely
sovereign in his administration of the covenant. The only place
where the human element comes in is in the response of faith to his
call and invitation. But covenant blessing is by faith alone, not
ancestry, not any ritual act, even the God-given covenant signs of
baptism and the Lord's Supper. That faith is itself the work of God,
part of the regeneration which is the essence of the mode of entering
the new covenant.

5. The child's relationship with God

With all these changes in the position of children under the new
covenant it is not surprising to find a change in this area too. In fact
it is not merely a change but something entirely new. For the fact is
that the relationship of the child to God is not even discussed in the
Old Testament. We see special children with a special relationship
with God, such as Isaac, Joseph, Moses, Samuel and David, because
they form links in the chain of the story of God's redemptive
purpose. But we have no idea how the normal child was to regard his
standing with God. His relationship with God is indirect — through
his parents who taught him the history and laws of Israel, exhorted
him to keep them and in due time to teach them to his own children
so that the covenant seed would continue. Jeremiah saw this indirect
knowledge of God as a mark of the old covenant in contrast with the
new.[23] Under the old covenant a man taught his neighbour or brother
to 'know the Lord'; under the new 'they will all know me, from **the
least of them** to the greatest'. Meanwhile, the least, such as children,
were dependent on their parents.

The coming of Jesus supplies what was lacking. The new
covenant relationship is direct — we are 'born of God' and become
his sons. No longer do we boast that 'we are Abraham's sons'; we
have a higher boast: 'I am a son of God'. We 'know him' at firsthand.
This enables us to answer the question: 'What about a child? Can a
child be a son of God in his own right?'

The best way to approach this question is to refer to the words of
Jesus in Mark 10:13-16.[24] The answer is found both in what Jesus
did and what he said; both his words and actions are significant. He
said and did things no rabbi ever would. He 'let the children come'
to him and gave them his personal and undivided attention. Acting
as God's Messiah he demonstrated that his kingdom and covenant

extended to them, even while they were still children: 'the kingdom of heaven belongs to such'. That is, the new covenant, by which a person has direct access to God, not mediated through parents, can include children. This is why he went further and embraced them. He did this as Messiah, for of him it was prophesied that he 'gathers the lambs in his arms and carries them close to his heart' (Isa. 40:11). Here is the promised Shepherd of Israel carrying out his mission.

His words confirm and enlarge on his actions, especially the statement 'the kingdom of God belongs to such as these.' By 'such as' (Greek *Toiouton*) he did not mean 'children as such, children as children', but those **like** children. This he made clear in the words, 'anyone who will not receive the kingdom of God **like a little child** will never enter it'. There are certain characteristics of a child that should mark the spirit of all who come to him. They come with a sense of weakness, helplessness and utter dependence. Luke describes them as 'babies' (Greek *brephe* not *paidia*). Who is more weak, helpless and dependent than a baby? Did not Jesus say that we must be born again and become babies to enter the kingdom?[25]

If then all must become childlike to enter the kingdom, it must be possible for a child to do so. If 'such as' children are welcome, then children themselves are. This surely answers the question whether a child can become a son of God in his own right and enter into a personal relationship with him. Clearly he can; and here we see the way in which his position in the new covenant most transcends that in the old. How an individual Israelite child thought or felt about God is something we are not told. The material we have about children points them to their parents. It is to them they direct their trust and obedience and it is from them they learn of God. Under the new covenant, as Isaiah 54:13 predicted: 'all your sons will be taught by the Lord'. That this includes children comes out plainly and powerfully in the incident recorded in Mark 10. For Jesus himself declared Isaiah's words fulfilled through him. After quoting them, he added, 'Everyone who listens to the Father and learns of him comes to me' (John 6:45).

The subject of the child's relationship with God will be given more extended treatment in a later section.

B. THEIR EDUCATION

Earlier we saw something of how children were educated in Old
Testament times. This too has been affected by the coming of Christ
with the new covenant or gospel, just as has their place in the scheme
of things generally. This can be looked at in three ways.

1. What they are educated for

Under the old covenant children's education was geared to their
place in the nation of Israel. They were important, indeed essential,
for the continuance of Israel as God's covenant people. God had
raised up this nation and entered into covenant with it. The time
would come when the way into this relationship would be opened up
to all nations, as he promised when he said to Abraham, 'all peoples
on earth will be blessed through you' (Gen. 12:3), but until that time
this knowledge would be confined to that one people. Since each
generation could not hope to last more than seventy or eighty years,
it was vital for the children to come to understand why and how they
belonged to a special people. Only thus could the covenant with
Israel continue until Messiah came. 'Your sons will take the place
of their fathers; you will make them princes throughout the land. I
will perpetuate your memory through all generations; therefore the
nations will praise you for ever and ever' (Ps. 45:16f).

Israelite children therefore were educated for their lives as God's
covenant people. They must learn who they were, what it meant to
be an Israelite and what was expected of them. They were therefore
taught the history and laws of Israel in order, as Psalm 45 says, 'to
take the place of their fathers'. Then in due course they would
educate their own children to take their place. The purpose of
education was to ensure the continuance of the covenant down the
generations until the Messiah came.

What do we find when we turn the pages of the New Testament?
What guidance do Christians have about the education of their
children? The answer is — not a lot. The New Testament says little
about children anyway and even less about their education. It's a
case of the dog that didn't bark — the silence is the significant factor.
The comparative silence of the New Testament on children does not
mean the Old Testament way is still in operation; it means we are in
a totally new situation. The old covenant has run its course and the

great promise to Abraham is being fulfilled; his blessing is coming to all nations. The new covenant is made, not with one nation, but with people in the whole world. On the day of its birth, when the Holy Spirit came down in visible and audible form, Peter declared that he (the Spirit) was being 'poured out on all people' (Acts 2:17). He invited those present from all parts of the empire to receive this gift by repenting of their rejection of their Messiah and publicly acknowledging him in baptism, adding, 'the promise is for you and your children and for all who are afar off — those whom the Lord our God shall call' (Acts 2:39). Those responding could teach their children about Jesus and the Spirit and invite them to receive their gifts. But they could do more. Since the promise was also for those 'far off', that is, people of other nations, their witness could go outside the home as well as within it, indeed it could extend beyond their frontiers.

It is from this principle we draw our deductions about the education of children in gospel times. This is no longer spelt out as it had been under the old covenant. How could it be when God's people are scattered throughout the world and not all assembled in one nation? God's people are in all the world and their children need to be educated to live in the world. It is a pluralist world, not one governed by the laws and teachings of God. It is a world of infinite variety in which each nation has its own history and culture. It is a world in which activities and opportunities differ from one place to another. If children are to be educated to live in this world they will have to be educated as those around them are. They will have to learn the history, customs and laws of their own nation. They will have to acquire knowledge which will enable them to play their part in the life of the nation, to earn a living in it and to perform some sort of service for it.

Yet this does not mean that our children become lost in a vast mass of the ungodly. For while the New Testament widens our boundaries it also narrows them. On one hand it speaks in terms of the world rather than one nation. But on the other it speaks in a way the Old Testament does not of the importance of each individual. Jesus declared his concern over 'one sinner who repents' (Matt. 18:12-14). When he turned his spotlight on the children he referred to them as individuals and warned against despising 'one of them' (Matt. 18:6,10). No longer do they exist for the sake of the family, clan or nation. They are important in their own right. But their importance lies not in linking one generation to the next but in serving as far as possible the whole of society, indeed the world itself. So they need to be taught, not only to receive the promise of God, but how to live in the world, because it is the environment in which they are to bear their witness.

2. Whom they are educated by

Nothing is clearer than that the entire education of Old Testament children was entrusted to their parents. They had been taught the basics by their own parents and their responsibility was to pass these on to their children. As has been seen, this involved telling them all it meant to be God's covenant people. At eight days they had circumcised their sons, and now they must show them just what that meant. They must pass on the stories which described the way they had become a special people and the laws that distinguished them from all other nations. To do this they required no specialised knowledge and no acquired skills. The task was well within the capacity of the Israelite parent. God would not have laid this duty on them if it had been beyond their capability. Nor did it require special buildings equipped with libraries and other educational resources. The home was adequate, and this was where it was carried out. 'These commandments that I give you today are to be upon your hearts. Impress them on your children. Talk about them when you **sit at home** and when you walk along the road, when you lie down and when you get up ... Write them on the door-frames of your houses and on your gates' (Deut. 6:6-9).

Education was very much a family affair. In due time these children would marry and they would have children. Even who they married was regulated by God's law. Abraham's concern that his son, the co-founder of the nation, should have a wife, not from the heathen tribes but from his own family, became an example for the whole nation to follow. When they deviated from this they were reproached and reminded that God wanted 'a godly offspring', which necessitated marriage within their own nation (Mal. 2:15).

Who educates the children of believers under the new covenant? The silence of the New Testament means we must draw our conclusions from the nature of the covenant itself. It has already been established that our children are being prepared for life in the world. The new covenant people of God is the church, and our children certainly have their place in that when they learn the truth that is in Jesus and come to personal faith in him. But this church connection forms only part of their lives, just as the church itself forms only a small section of society. They will grow up to live in a community in which the majority of households make no profession of Christ. Most of them will pursue their careers in institutions owned and controlled by non-Christians. If they are to be happy in such a situation and to prosper, they must be educated for it. They will therefore need to be taught subjects, disciplines and skills which are far beyond the capacity of their parents. They will need professional teachers trained for such a task, the same teachers as those who teach non-Christians. This calls for schools, colleges and universities outside the home, equipped with all the necessary resources. Education for life in the world means education with and by the world.

When the gospel was taken out of Jerusalem into the world it did not remove believers from their communities into a separate Christian environment. While it changed their thinking, experience and behaviour, it left them with the same pattern of life. They used the same shops and plied the same trades (except where persecution made this impossible). They also attended the same schools and universities, which existed all over the Roman Empire. There is no evidence that Christians either withdrew their children to educate them at home or set up their own special institutions. Parents would have needed to monitor what was taught, especially where it included pagan philosophy. But since they had already imbibed this themselves and come to see where it was contrary to Christian doctrine, they would readily be able to explain it to their children. There was no reason why their children should not know what the philosophers taught, even if it was unacceptable to Christians. In fact there was every reason why they **should** know it, since it shaped the thinking of those among whom they were being prepared to witness the gospel.

There is no reason why this pattern should not have continued down the centuries and still persist today. It is true that churches opened schools, but this was usually where no one else was attending to the education of children. There were of course those churches that set up schools for the purpose of indoctrination, but the spirit of the Reformation was against this.

There may be circumstances in which the world's education becomes so bad that Christians dare not entrust their children to it. Some feel that point has been reached in some schools in Britain today. They find themselves unable in all conscience to expose their children to the materialistic outlook that underlies much education today, with its assumption that evolution is a proven fact. They find that what passes for 'Religious Education' undermines their own presentation of the truth of the Bible to their children. In some instances lax discipline and low moral standards are having an adverse effect on their children. Some find their children are learning very little at all, and that they could manage the job better themselves. Such have excellent reasons for considering withdrawing their children from the State system and educating them at home or co-operating in setting up schools controlled by Christians.

This however is the pragmatic approach, not based on a theological principle of education derived from the New Testament. There are also those who are guided to this segregation by the Old Testament principle outlined earlier. These would probably educate their children outside the State system, however good it was. But if we follow the logic of our new covenant theology, it means that, apart from exceptionally bad circumstances, education for the world means education by the world.

3. What they are educated in

As already seen, Old Testament parents had the duty of preparing their children for life in the covenant community. This meant telling them the nation's **history**, how it originated and came to possess that land. Further, it meant teaching the **laws** by which God governed his special people. But the education process had to go beyond merely teaching what these laws were; it meant teaching them to **observe** these laws. This had always been obligatory, right from the time of Abraham, of whom God said, 'I have chosen him so that he will direct his children and his household after him to keep the way of the Lord by doing what is right and just, so that the Lord will bring about for Abraham what he has promised him' (Gen. 18:19). When that promise was fulfilled and the nation stood on the threshold of the land, he directed all parents through Moses to do as Abraham had done.[26] Since what Moses was impressing on the parents was not just knowledge of the law but obedience to it, it would be this that they were to teach their children.[27] This became so much the pattern of the life of Israel that it actually became a subject of psalm-singing when David later established public worship.[28]

The fact was that parents were responsible for their children's behaviour. The father had to answer for the sins and crimes of his children. It was therefore in the parents' interest to train their children well, so that they could assume responsibility for their own behaviour as they grew up: 'Train a child in the way he should go, and when he is old he will not turn from it' (Prov. 22:6). Then the parent was released from his responsibility. So children had to learn right from wrong and acquire the necessary self-control to apply this distinction to their behaviour. To achieve this, children were to be trained above all else in three things:

a. Obedience to parents. Everything depended on this, as the fifth commandment shows.[29] Not only was this principle written on stone tablets by the finger of God along with the great duties of worshipping him and refraining from major crimes like murder, adultery and theft, but to it was attached the promise of the tenure of the land. Unless each generation observed the laws of the covenant it could not continue to live in the promised land. Since it was parents who taught these laws it was they who must first be obeyed. There are many references to this obedience and the seriousness of not rendering it, in the law code of Exodus and Deuteronomy. Proverbs also lays great stress on it. Indeed the book as a whole is a manual of what parents were to teach their children under the old covenant.

b. Right and wrong company. Proverbs puts this high on the list of what parents should teach their children. After the introduction it immediately launches into this subject. Children as they grew up were to avoid getting mixed up with such as muggers, highwaymen and prostitutes. For even in the theocratic nation with its perfect laws there were 'the wicked'. The law did not change hearts, neither did circumcision. There were always those who despised it and even misled their children. With such as these the obedient child was to have nothing to do.

c. How to please God. The body of the Book of Proverbs sets down the type of behaviour that pleases or displeases God. The style of the main part of the book is 'antithetic', that is, the second member of each verse contrasts with the first. This helped memorisation at a time when families did not possess written Scriptures. So one generation passed on to the next what it had learned by heart from its parents. This was what education was all about in old covenant Israel.

What then of 'the new Israel', the Church of Christ? Christian parents will certainly teach their children the new covenant or gospel in the way Israelites taught theirs the old covenant. They will tell them the stories of Jesus who came to seek a people for himself from all nations. They will teach them how to please God and especially about obedience to parents, as Paul instructed in Ephesians 6:1-4 and Colossians 3:20. They will do all they can to protect them while in their tender state, remembering what Jesus said about their vulnerability.[30] But all this will be looked at in a later section.

Here we are concerned with education in the wider sense. On this the New Testament says nothing. The matter is left open. But since our children are, as we have seen, to be educated for and by the world, they will need educating in the things of the world. All subjects and skills are open to them. There are no specifically 'Christian' subjects apart from the Bible itself and what pertains to it. To put it another way, all subjects are 'Christian'. From our God has come this vast creation with all its marvels. From our God has come man with all his skills. History is the story of God's providential acts. To study any subject connected with those things is to study the ways of God. The child who is being taught the truths of God at home will learn to see him in everything he encounters. He will not need to have special Christian teachers to do this for him. It is a bonus if his teachers are Christians but it is not essential. Even if they are, it is far better for him to work out for himself how his subject relates to God than be spoonfed or indoctrinated by someone else.

A liberal education is part of the liberty enjoyed by New Testament believers who are freed from the law. The gospel has such power to change human nature that everything with which that new nature comes into contact is transformed in its eyes. Very young children need protection. They also need to learn obedience. The parent who gives the protection is trusted, and the obedience comes willingly, just as believers obey God cheerfully because they know they can trust him. Once rooted in this trust and obedience 'the plants' are ready to be brought from the hothouse into the open air. They can view the world and receive the education it offers. It will be they who influence the world not the world them.

Even in Old Testament times we find hints of this. There were some who from early days were wrenched from their godly homes and brought up among the Gentiles. Moses, Joseph and Daniel are the most notable cases. Being 'in the world' they were educated in the wisdom and culture of nations such as Egypt and Babylon. This played a great part in equipping them for the tasks they had to perform of showing the leaders and people of those nations the power and righteousness of God.

So what we are saying is: (i) that education under the new covenant has similarities with that under the old. Christian parents teach their children the new covenant (gospel) as Israelite parents taught theirs the old (law). We teach them how to become children of God through Christ, how to please Christ, beginning with learning obedience to us as parents. All this is done by parents in the home as it was in Israel.

But (ii) we are also saying that there are differences that arise from the change of covenant. Our children are not growing up to serve a godly nation but an ungodly world, in which they must find their way. We cannot keep them in ignorance of it nor from contact with it for ever. Nor should we try to. For Christians are 'in the world' (John 17:11,15,18). The sanctifying work of God gives protection from its evil. Nothing else can, even our attempts at sheltering them.[31] They must circulate among the people of the world and find their place among them. So their education needs to be as wide as possible. They must go out of their homes and be exposed to the world. Parents are not equipped to give them what they need. But at the same time as this process is going on they will continue to enjoy the benefits of a godly home. The two can work very well together.

References

Section 1, Part II, A
1   Rom. 6:1
2   Gen. 4:1; 48:9; Ps. 45:16f; 127:3; 144:12
3   Gen. 16:1-6; 30:2; 1 Sam. 1:8-11
4   Matt. 5:1-12
5   Luke 6:20-23
6   Matt. 5:11f
7   e.g. Eph. 1:3ff
8   Matt. 10:21,35-37
9   Mark 7:24-30; 9:21-27; John 4:46-54
10 John 16:20-22
11 Matt. 19:3-10
12 Matt. 19:11-12
13 1 Cor. 7:7,32-35
14 1 Cor. 7:1-6
15 1 Cor. 7:24,27
16 Deut. 25:5f
17 1 Tim. 1:3
18 Phil. 3:4-11
19 1 Thess. 1:10; 2 Thess. 2:5
20 Rev. 22:3
21 Jer. 31:33a,34
22 Ezek. 36:25f
23 Jer. 31:34
24 See also Matt. 18:1-3;19:13f; Luke 18:15-17
25 A fuller discussion on this passage will be given on pp. 72-76
Section 1, Part II, B
26 Deut. 4:8-10;6:6f
27 Deut. 4:1f, 5f
28 Ps. 78:1-8
29 Exod. 20:12
30 Matt. 18:6
31 John 17:15-17

Section II:
The child's relationship with God

Part 1:
The child's nature

'Few Christian parents', wrote Ron Buckland, 'seem to have an assured understanding of their own children's status before God. This comment applies equally to churches in which infant baptism is practised and those in which believers' baptism is the norm. It seems that within the church as a whole there is no settled "theology of childhood"'.[1] It is indeed a fact that Christians are often uncertain as to how to treat their children: should they teach them to pray to God as their heavenly Father and to sing hymns which express knowledge of Jesus and faith in him? Or should they treat them as ignorant sinners who can only be evangelised and urged to repentance and faith? The way we teach them to think and act towards God will depend on how we view them, on what we think is their relation to God and their status in his kingdom.

To discover the Bible's teaching on a child's relationship to God involves looking at a number of issues, which can be grouped under the headings of its **nature** and its **salvation**. In this chapter we consider **the child's nature**.

A. SIN

The question at issue is whether all children irrespective of their parentage are by nature sinners and therefore lost from God. Is a child a sinner? If so, in what sense? Without going outside the evangelical constituency it is possible to find a number of different answers to this question.

1. All children belong to Christ until they reject him

This is stated by John Inchley in *Realities of Childhood* thus: 'all children have the spiritual status of belonging to the Lord until such time as they deliberately reject him'.[2] This author does not himself face the question as to whether or in what sense children are sinners, but quotes another writer, George Goodman, who comes nearer to it. In *The Heathen, their present state and future*, he wrote: 'all irresponsible persons (infants and others) will have no charge against them and can therefore be the objects of that free grace that comes through the reconciliation made at Calvary. The gifts of salvation and eternal life may justly be extended to them since where there is no law there is no transgression (Rom. 4:15; 5:13)'.[3]

Although terms like 'reconciliation' and 'salvation' seem to imply that children are in need of these and therefore in sin, this is virtually denied by the allusion to Paul's words in Romans (which are incompletely quoted). The interpretation seems to be that a child does not become a sinner until it consciously and deliberately commits an act of sin. This is borne out by Inchley's development of Goodman's teaching, in which he refers to John 3:16-21 and Revelation 20:15, saying, 'those for whom the second death has power are the rejecters of Christ — those who have loved darkness instead of light'.[4]

Another writer to whom Inchley appeals is the great Anglican evangelical theologian W. H. Griffith-Thomas who, in commenting on Article 27 ('Of Baptism'), says: 'What is the spiritual position of these infants in relation to our Lord? Surely the truth is that all children are included in the great atoning sacrifice and belong to Jesus Christ until they deliberately reject him'.[5] Although writing on the subject of infant baptism and therefore to Christians, he does not seem to qualify 'all children' and thus includes those of unbelievers, atheists, Satanists, Muslims, Hindus, idolaters and so on.

A later writer who appears to go along with Inchley is Ron Buckland who makes much of the fact that Inchley's view is based on the words of Jesus in Mark 10:13-16, especially, 'let the little children come unto me and do not hinder them, for the kingdom of God belongs to such as these'. Like Inchley, Buckland believes that 'all children are in God's kingdom until they opt out',[6] for he writes, 'Jesus teaches that children already belong to the kingdom of God'.[7] He realises that this raises the question of a child's involvement in the Fall, particularly in view of what Paul wrote in Romans 3:23 and 5:12. Rejecting the term 'original sin' because it is Augustinian rather than Pauline, he prefers to phrase the problem 'How are children involved in the rebellion of Adam?'[8] He questions whether children are guilty and accountable in the same sense as adults: 'It seems reasonable to say that when a child can have a conscious experience of sin he can have a conscious experience of guilt. Before that he lacks understanding'.[9]

Unfortunately in using words like 'aware' and 'experience' Buckland is not really facing the question of a child's **status** before God, only its conscious **feelings**. However, since he is clear that 'all children begin with God',[10] he does not see sin as an actual condition, only a potential one. Belonging to the kingdom is 'a belongingness that may become rebellion. This answer takes account of humanity's rebellion against God and the child's potential to be part of that rebellion'.[10] But it will only become 'part of that rebellion' if later it 'consciously says "No" to Jesus'.[11] 'Another way ... is to say that God views each child with favour and that this favour continues until the child turns his back on it'.[12]

Both Inchley and Buckland write under the auspices of Scripture Union, possibly our leading evangelical agency in child evangelism. In spite of the disclaimer, their position indicates some change in the theology of that body from that which pertained in earlier days. This view is expressed by a former leading light in Scripture Union, R. Hudson Pope: 'If we want to know what the heart of an unsaved child is like, we shall find the answer in our Lord's own words in Mark 7:21 — "For from within, out of the heart of man, proceed evil thoughts, adulteries, fornications, murders, thefts, covetousness, wickedness, deceit, lasciviousness, an evil eye, blasphemy, pride, foolishness." This is our Lord's picture of the human heart, and the heart of a child, for he makes no age limit'.[13] Buckland himself quotes this alongside the Inchley view. The two positions lead to different ways of approaching children: those who adopt the first will have as their objective 'to elicit a response of repentance and faith in the light of the awful consequences of the child's sinful state'. Those who follow the latter will see themselves as 'helping children to understand what it means to belong to Jesus'.[14] The question of status is therefore vital to the whole matter of how we treat our children spiritually. Every one of us must decide whether the 'all children belong to Jesus Christ until they deliberately refuse him' position is the biblical one or not.

2. The children of believing parents belong to God by virtue of their parentage

Ron Buckland states this position in these words: 'the presence of at least one Christian parent cancels out the consequences of a child's sinful nature'.[15] It is difficult to discover the source of this view and it is not his own position. Plenty of support can be found for the way he continues: 'The thinking behind this answer is based on biblical teaching about the covenant ... Those who become part of this covenant become the people of God. The children are born into this status. So, when Paul says in 1 Corinthians 7:14: "Otherwise your children would be unclean, but as it is, they are holy", this can be interpreted as teaching that children gain right standing before the holy God because at least one of their parents is a believer'.[15]

Many evangelical and particularly Reformed commentators see the children of believers as included in the covenant between God and his people and therefore as having a place in the church. Some go further and claim this gives such children the right to baptism. Many too interpret 1 Corinthians 7:14 in this way. But they do not even discuss how this affects the child's inherited sinful condition. One who does and who gets nearest to Buckland's statement is Calvin himself. In his commentary on 1 Corinthians 7:14, after saying that 'the children of believers are set apart from others by a certain special privilege, so that they are regarded as holy in the church', he opens a discussion on how this harmonises with Ephesians 2:3, that we are 'all by nature children of wrath', and Psalm 51:5: 'Behold I was conceived of sin'. First he affirms 'that there is a universal propagation both of sin and condemnation in the seed of Adam ... all are included in this curse, whether they spring from believers or the ungodly'. However, Paul has declared they are 'holy through the blessing of the covenant *by whose intervention the curse of nature is destroyed* ... Those who were by nature unclean are consecrated to God by his grace ... *Children of believers are made exempt from the common condition of mankind in order to be set apart for the Lord*'.[16]

Before assuming that Calvin teaches the cancellation of the consequences of a child's sinful nature we should note what he says in the *Institutes* on the transmission of sin. There he appears to attribute the view he expressed in the commentary on 1 Corinthians

7:14 to Pelagius 'who holds it unlikely that children should derive
corruption from godly parents inasmuch as the offspring ought to be
sanctified by the parents' purity (cf. 1 Cor. 7:14)'.[17] He allies
himself rather with Augustine who taught 'whether a man is a guilty
unbeliever or an innocent believer he begets not innocent but guilty
children, for he begets them from a corrupted nature'. He then
qualifies this statement with the words, 'Now it is a special blessing
of God's people that they partake in some degree of their parents'
holiness'.

He does not define that 'degree', but those who have followed
Calvin see it more as an outward status than an inward change of
state. Pierre Marcel, who quotes Calvin at length, describes it as 'an
objective theocratic holiness ... by the privilege of the covenant'.[18]
John Murray calls it 'the holiness of connection and privilege ... that
evinces the operation of the covenant'.[19] F. W. Grosheide says
'"Holy", used of the children as a group, has the same meaning as
"sanctified" or "holy" when used of the people of Israel'.[20] Calvin
therefore may simply have meant that the natural sinfulness of all
children does not prevent their being included in the covenant and
thus received into the congregation of a Christian church. They still
need regeneration but prior to that experience they truly belong to
God. Perhaps this is what Buckland means by saying that a Christian
parent 'cancels out the **consequences** of the child's sinful nature'.
There seems to be no authority for saying that children of believing
parents are born without a sinful nature, nor that the covenant
cancels it out. Even Roman Catholicism does not go this far since it
would surely impinge on their view of the immaculate conception
of Mary.

3. All children begin life outside the kingdom of God.

David Kingdon meets our question head on: 'All men without
exception are born in union with Adam ... In union with Adam all
die, for in him all sinned (Rom. 5:12) ... To maintain that children
are not born in Adam and thus are not subject from birth to
condemnation and death is to deny the plain teaching of Scripture.
Birth connection with Christian parents does not and cannot translate a child from union with Adam into union with Christ ... Every
child of man is born into the Adamic race. If there were exceptions
to this rule it would follow that death has not passed on all, but only

some (Rom. 5:12)'.[21] From this he concludes the absolute necessity of regeneration for children, basing his claim on John 3:6 and 1 Corinthians 15:50.

Recent evangelical writers on children have problems with this position. Ron Buckland, for example, with reference to this teaching though not to David Kingdon specifically, says, 'There are enormous problems with applying this teaching to young children'. One problem is that it means calling them to repentance and faith. 'It is not clear how we can talk about repentance and faith in a child who is not yet capable of language, much less comprehension'.[22] Another is that it is difficult to square with the view expressed under '1.', which Buckland holds, that the kingdom belongs to little children.

These problems lead him to question the concept of 'original sin' although he claims only to be attacking the phrase and not the teaching. The phrase is not to be found in the Bible but was coined by Augustine in the fourth century. However, whatever the teaching is called he does not identify with it, but puts forward the view, already stated, that 'all children begin with God but will drift from that position unless an effective nurturing or evangelistic influence operates in their lives'.[23] It is if and when that point of drifting is reached that children 'become involved in the rebellion of Adam'. Although he does not deny the so-called 'original sin' teaching, he clearly cannot hold this and the view that 'all children begin with God' at the same time.

Mr Buckland's position is interesting. It appears that the practical problem of requiring repentance and faith from young children has led him to query the theological question of the Bible's teaching on their state and status. Theology says that 'from conception the child is sinful because he is human ... But what if the child is not aware of this? Is the child accountable to God? It seems reasonable to say that when a child can have a conscious experience of sin he can have a conscious experience of guilt'.[24] If this represents current evangelical thinking on the status of children then it is clear that thinking has moved from a theological to a pragmatic approach. We are asked to begin with what children can 'feel' and 'experience' not from biblical teaching.

A similar approach underlies the Freudianism which has given the whole idea of guilt such a bad press for the past century. The attention has been concentrated on 'guilt feelings'. Freud's mission was to deliver his patients from these feelings which had been generated by certain experiences in childhood, and to remove the sense of guilt which was the cause of their mental illness. The current evangelical mission is to see children safe in Christ without arousing these guilt feelings. In the years prior to the age of discretion they are incapable of such feelings anyway, and if we have to wait for them there will be a whole period in which they must be seen as unsaved. So we dispense with feelings. Then, after the years of discretion have arrived they need no guilt feelings since they are in the kingdom unless and until they consciously reject it. If that happens they will need to be encouraged to repent of that rejection and to come back to Christ.

This is a new approach within evangelicalism and is connected with a misunderstanding of the Pauline teaching as summarised by David Kingdon. It fails to see that for Paul guilt is not a feeling but a status. Perhaps Augustine has misled us by inventing the terms 'original sin' and 'original guilt'. We get nearer to the New Testament by talking about 'imputed guilt', and saying that the responsibility for Adam's transgression is **laid to the account** of all who are descended from him. This means two things: i) that our guilt is a reality whether or not we ever commit a blameworthy act; ii) that we are in a state of guilt whether or not we experience guilt feelings.

This is very relevant to new-born children who clearly have committed no blameworthy acts or experienced guilty feelings. It concentrates our minds on the theological rather than the pragmatic. What we must decide before we address matters of a child's conscious conviction or response is whether this is the teaching of the New Testament.

This takes us back to Romans 5:12-21. Paul is explaining his teaching on justification, which has occupied him since the middle of chapter 1. He has been trying to show that we are made right with God by believing in Christ's atoning sacrifice. Through this the righteousness of Christ is 'imputed' to us, that is, reckoned, credited or put down to our account.[25] In chapter 5 he further clarifies this by bringing out the parallel between our new relationship to Christ through faith and our old relationship with Adam through birth. So he begins verse 12 with 'just as', although he breaks off after verse 12 to explain something very important for the question we are addressing, and doesn't resume until verse 18 where he comes back to his 'just as'.

But our interest is mainly in verses 12-14, our state due to our descent from Adam, because this applies directly to children. What Adam did was to bring sin into the world (v. 12). This **could** mean that from that time acts of sin were possible to anyone, that everyone comes here like Adam faced with a choice between obedience and disobedience. Some take this view, which constitutes the area of dispute between Augustine and Pelagius. However, Paul does not mean that, for he says 'because all sinn**ed**', not 'all **may** sin' or 'all **do** sin'. Before any conscious choice to sin or not is made, sin has been committed. That distinction was drawn in 3:23 — what unites humanity is sin, in the two senses: having 'sinned' (a past act), and 'falling short of the glory of God' (a present act, or series of acts). That this past act of sin which everyone has committed is Adam's original transgression is clear from the phrases used in verses 15-20: 'the trespass of one man' (v. 15), 'the one man's sin ... one sin' (v. 16), 'the trespass of the one man' (v. 17), 'one trespass' (v. 18), 'the disobedience of the one man' (v. 19) and 'the trespass' (v. 20). All this relates to what he said in verse 14 about Adam having sinned 'by breaking a command'. That sin of Adam recorded in Genesis 3 was the past act of sin we have all committed.

The parallel he draws with the righteous act of Christ shows in what sense he regards us as having sinned. For he has already said that Christ's act of obedience to death on the cross has been 'credited' to us by faith (4:24). It shows up on our account with God. The same applies to our state in sin. He is not saying we all do what Adam did. True as this may be it is not that which constitutes us sinners. He is saying that Adam's sin was 'charged to us', it shows up on our account. It is cancelled out when through faith Christ's righteous sacrifice is put down on our account. The merit of his act is more than enough to pay off our debt inherited from Adam.

But must we apply this to children, even babies? The answer lies in the fact of death. Death is the divine punishment for sin,[26] the 'wages' it earns.[27] The punishment proves the offence — those who die must have sinned or they would not die. All do die, therefore all have sinned: 'death came to all men because all sinned' (v. 12). It is at this point Paul breaks into his analogy. Instead of balancing his 'just as' with a 'so also', he has to clarify the position beyond all possible doubt and without any exception. Some might ask: does this apply to Gentiles, to the ignorant, to infants, or perhaps imbeciles, all who do not know 'the law', that is, what God requires and commands, what is right and what is wrong, all who for one reason or another cannot respond? The answer (v. 13) is that sin existed and exists apart from law: 'before the law was given sin was in the world'. How can this be, since law defines what sin is: 'sin is the transgression of the law' (1 John 3:4, A.V.), and 'sin is not taken into account when there is no law'? Those who sinned before the law came in or came to them cannot be held to account. But they **were** held to account! And punished! They died! 'Nevertheless death reigned from the time of Adam to the time of Moses.' People died who had not broken a revealed law, who had not even done what Adam did! God gave him a command and he broke it, and deserved what he got. But these have not done so. Yet they are punished with death. Why?

There can only be one answer. They were charged with Adam's sin. The proof? 'Adam was the pattern of the one to come' (v. 14), the one who would put everything right by a righteous act which he would put down to the account of all who believe in him, thus wiping their slate clean.

The condition of our children then is clear. They are in a state of sin and death. The fact that many die in the womb or infancy proves this. This is the theology of Paul. It raises what Buckland calls 'enormous problems': what if they die before they hear of Christ? How can they feel guilty, repent and believe during their infancy? But the problems must not dictate the theology. This seems to be the tendency that has developed in the current theology of children. The problems are insoluble, therefore the theology must be wrong. This is putting the cart before the horse. We must get the theology right then face the problems. Which is what we will try to do.

B. RESPONSIBILITY

The terms 'responsibility' and 'accountability' have cropped up several times in the course of discussing sin, and must now be carefully examined. Reference was made earlier to the view of John Inchley and George Goodman that children are in the kingdom unless and until they say 'No' to Christ. In the course of stating their case they used the word 'irresponsible' of children: 'All irresponsible persons (infants and others) will have no charge against them ... Children are irresponsible persons until they are mature enough to make a meaningful choice to receive or reject the Saviour for themselves'.[28] According to this view there is a period in life in which a child is not only **unable** to respond to the call of Christ but not **required** to do so. During this period it is not necessary for it to be conscious of sin and guilt for it does not have to confess and repent.

This raises the whole question of responsibility and accountability in childhood, not only in relation to the gospel but to the law. For there are two aspects of responsibility: moral — responsibility to the law; and spiritual — responsibility to the gospel; the demand of God to answer for your own sin, and the demand of Christ to answer his call. What does Scripture say about this?

As regards the Old Testament, the issue is not explicitly discussed, but there are indications that young children were not held morally responsible for their behaviour. 'The child', writes Pridmore, 'is set in a category apart from that of the adult in that he cannot be held morally responsible for his actions'.[29] This deduction is drawn mainly from two passages. First, Deuteronomy 1:39: 'Your children who do not yet know good from bad ...' These are distinguished from the adult generation of Israelites who were held responsible for their rebellion and punished with death in the desert outside the promised land. Second, Isaiah 7:15f: 'He will eat curds and honey when he knows enough to reject the wrong and choose the right. But before the boy knows enough to reject the wrong and choose the right ...' This indicates a time when a child lacks moral awareness. Before that time is reached, says Isaiah, Israel's enemies will be destroyed. Putting the two passages together we have the two ideas of lack of moral awareness and also of responsibility. But nowhere in the Old Testament do we find any indication of a specific age at which this moral awareness dawns in a child.

The fact that children lacked a sense of moral awareness for a period did not mean they were regarded as being in a state of innocence. In fact the opposite appears to be the case. It indicates they are born in a state of blindness resulting from their participation in the Fall, and that like blind persons they are inclined to blunder and stumble. A bias towards sin quickly develops: 'Even from the birth the wicked go astray; from the womb they are wayward and speak lies' (Ps. 58:3). So serious is this condition that even the Flood failed to remove it, as God himself admitted after it was over: 'Never again will I curse the ground because of man, even though every inclination of his heart is evil from his childhood' (Gen. 8:21). This is very little different from his state before the Flood: 'Every inclination of the thoughts of his heart was only evil all the time' (Gen. 6:5). The Flood proves that evil is inborn in human nature.

According to Pridmore the word used for 'children' in Isaiah 3:4 ('I will make boys their officials and mere children will govern them') is derived from a word meaning 'to act wantonly for one's own pleasure', indicating the capriciousness of the child left to himself.[30] This is the condition Proverbs seeks to obviate, written as it was primarily for 'the simple' (1:4). The word is not used in a pejorative sense of mental deficiency, for its basic meaning is 'open'. Children of tender years have formed no definite ideas or opinions but are still 'open' to instruction. The 'simple' are those who are uninstructed, they are ignorant of God's requirements, as they are of the dangers from people around them and of their own potentiality to follow evil examples. They must be taught so that this bias can be corrected and they can be directed into right paths. Thus Proverbs is full of righteous precepts and warnings against evil thoughts and actions.

Notwithstanding all this Israelite children were still seen as belonging to God: 'Yet you brought me out of the womb, you made me trust in you even at my mother's breast' (Ps. 22:9f); 'My frame was not hidden from you when I was made in the secret place. When I was woven together in the depths of the earth, your eyes saw my unformed body. All the days ordained for me were written in your book before one of them came to be' (Ps. 139:15f). The reason for this, as discussed in the first chapter, is that they were born of parents in covenant with God, and through circumcision they too had entered that relationship.

This indicates the way this condition of ignorance plus a bias to sin could be met. Children would be taught by their parents, and their first lesson was to obey them, as set down in the fifth commandment. This commandment is placed between the direct duties to God (1-4) and those to man (6-10). Whilst this has led to disagreement as to which of the two tables of the law it belongs to, it does show how central and pivotal it was. We have already considered the duty of parents to teach their children and have seen how they were held responsible for their children's behaviour until they became sufficiently responsible to answer for their own actions. Parents grounded their children in the Torah with their eyes on the day when the child would be sufficiently instructed to take the burden of responsibility from the parent and on to itself. Later Judaism fixed a date for this — at age thirteen, and marked it with a special ceremony, the Bar-mitzvah ('son of the law'), but this was unknown during the period to which the Old Testament Scriptures relate. No doubt it was more realistic not to fix an age, for growth to moral responsibility is a gradual process and varies from child to child.

We have also seen how vital this training period was to the people of Israel, because God dealt with the nation as a whole, either for blessing or cursing. Each generation had to learn his ways if the nation was to continue to enjoy the blessings of the land. This is why the second commandment speaks of God as 'punishing the children for the sins of the father' (Exod. 20:5). This did not mean that individuals or even the authorities were permitted to wreak vengeance on children or bring them to justice, which was absolutely forbidden by the Torah.[31] Thus we read of Amaziah, a law-abiding king, refusing to execute the sons of his father's murderers, for which public opinion might have been lobbying, because the law was clear on the matter.[32] Only the God of perfect justice had the right to do something so drastic. To balance this was his promise of long life in the land for a generation whose parents had taught their children to obey the law.[33] Thus one generation could make or break another: an older generation could bring a curse on a succeeding one; or a rising generation could blight the whole nation. On the other hand if parents obeyed God and taught their children to obey them, then the blessing would continue.[34]

We however do not live under that covenant, which has been rescinded and given way to the new covenant; we are members not of the kingdom of Israel but the kingdom of God. So the question is: how much of all this still pertains? One thing is clear: God no longer judges one generation for the sins of an earlier one, or particular children for the crimes of their parents. This is spelt out in Ezekiel 18 in great detail. Ezekiel was one of the prophets of the new covenant, which he was predicting in that chapter. The principle of solidarity was to give way to that of individuality, not only in judgement but in blessing, as his thirty-sixth chapter declares, especially verses 25-27. In Jeremiah, the two ideas are brought into close juxtaposition: the principle of judging one generation for the sins of an earlier one is abolished in Jeremiah 31:29-30, which is immediately followed by the announcement of the new covenant, the gospel, which the Messiah would bring.[35]

But this still leaves open the question of the child's personal responsibility. On this it appears that the Old Testament idea of a period in which a child is seen as not morally or spiritually responsible still stands. For the coming of the kingdom and the new covenant has not altered the nature of a child as it comes into the world. Children always have and always will be 'inclined to evil from childhood'. What they were after the Fall, before and after the Flood they are still after Calvary.

However, the New Testament is a little more enlightening because it speaks of the existence of a basic moral sense in human nature even in those ignorant of the law: 'When the Gentiles who do not have the law, do by nature things required by the law, they are a law for themselves, even though they do not have the law, since they show that the requirements of the law are written on their hearts, their consciences also bearing witness, and their thoughts now accusing, now even defending them' (Rom. 2:14f).

While conscience is mentioned in several places in the Old Testament, we are not given the insight into it that we find in the above passage. But this does not mean we are to look on children now as morally responsible, unlike Old Testament times. The blindness is still there, for those spoken of as 'showing that the requirements of the law are written on their hearts' are the very people described in Romans 1 as idolaters, immoral and depraved. [56] The lack of moral awareness is still there. Conscience alone is inadequate; it needs instruction and guidance, otherwise a person will follow his natural bias to evil.

Who then gives this instruction under the new covenant? As before, it is still the parents, according to Paul in Ephesians 6:1-4. Clearly the idea of the family lies outside all covenant relationship; it is older and more basic than the Torah, and is just as relevant under the gospel. Moral instruction still comes down from parents to children. This is why Proverbs is still a useful book, if carefully interpreted. Children still need to be taught morality, to say nothing of the way of salvation. There is no more of a natural tendency towards these now than there ever was. The period of 'moral irresponsibility', if that is the right way to describe it, is still there.

At what point it ceases and passes from parents to children is something that cannot be fixed. It comes gradually and differs from one to another. 'Do it because I say so' gradually becomes 'Do it because it's right, because God approves, it accords with his word, it is helpful not harmful to others.' 'The concept summarised in the phrase "age of accountability" is not static. It is dynamic and complex, and includes the fact of individual differences'.[37]

The situation then seems to be that, while children are held responsible for the sin of Adam from birth or even conception,[38] they are not responsible for their own actions until they come to understand the difference between right and wrong and can make their own choices. The first choice is whether to obey their parents or not. Gradually they come to see there are more serious issues such as truth and honesty over which they must make choices. Once they see this they become responsible for the choices they make about them. Parents will need to be very sensitive to this process of development, so that they can know when to graduate from 'Do it because I say so' to deeper reasons. They also need to be able to discern when the child understands the rightness or wrongness of particular actions enough to be accountable for them. Then comes the time, as far as Christian parents are concerned, for opening up the subjects of confession, repentance and faith in Christ. However, this is to anticipate a later discussion. We still need to know more about how a child stands with God in the period prior to the awakening of responsibility. After all, the child may never reach that time.

C. DEATH

What happens to a child who dies in infancy, before it reaches the state of responsibility by which it can understand and respond to the law and the gospel? Since it is still held responsible for the sin of Adam, is it condemned to everlasting punishment? To this question different answers have been given.

1. The children of godly or believing parents are saved

In the seventeenth century Samuel Rutherford was frequently called on to counsel parents who had suffered the loss of young children. In 1637 he wrote to one such lady: 'If the Lord take any of them (your children) home to his house before the storm come on, take it well. The owner of the orchard may take down two or three apples off his own trees before midsummer, and ere they get the harvest sun. And it would not be seemly that his servant, the gardener, should chide him for it. Let our Lord pluck his own fruit at any season he pleaseth.

They are not lost to you; but are laid up so well as that they are coffered in heaven, where our Lord's best jewels lie'.[39] Although he does not specify the ages of the children nor whether they were old enough to profess faith, the likelihood is that the ground of the assurance he gives that the children are in heaven is the faith of the parent, for this was the prevailing view, as expressed in the Articles of the Synod of Dort, 1615:

'Seeing that we are to judge of the will of God by his word, which testifies that the children of believers are holy, not indeed by nature, but by the benefit of the gracious covenant, in which they are comprehended along with their parents; pious parents ought not to doubt of the election and salvation of their children, whom God hath called in infancy out of this life'.[40]

These divines based their view on an interpretation of the words of 1 Corinthians 7:14 ('your children are holy') discussed earlier. Rutherford was not a member of the Synod of Dort, but did attend the Westminster Assembly in 1643-7. This body did not endorse the unequivocal language of Dort but played safe:

'Elect infants, dying in infancy, are regenerated and saved by Christ through the Spirit, who worketh when and where and how he pleaseth. So also are all other elect persons who are incapable of being outwardly called by the ministry of the word'.[41]

This does not specifically state that the children of believers are 'elect', as Dort does, only that children who are 'elect' are also 'saved'.

This clause was adopted verbatim by the Congregational churches in their Savoy Declaration of 1658, in spite of its lack of clarity as to whether all children born of Christian parents are to be seen as 'elect', and whether any not so born may be elect. This may have limited its usefulness in pastoring the bereaved and led to the broadening of it in the ages following these Confessions, as seen in the second view.

2. All dying in infancy are saved

The first great document to express this position was the Baptist Confession, completed in 1677 but not published until 1689, which follows the Westminster Confession very closely except in matters to do with the covenant, baptism and children. The relevant clause is amended thus:

'Infants dying in infancy are regenerated and saved by Christ through the Spirit; who worketh when and where and how he pleaseth; so also are all elect persons, who are incapable of being outwardly called by the ministry of the word'.[42]

The important difference from Westminster is the omission of the word 'elect' before 'infants'. It may be argued that its retention in the second part covers this since infants are among those 'incapable of being outwardly called by the ministry of the word'. This indicates there is no departure from the Westminster doctrine of election on the part of the Baptists. They did however differ from the Presbyterians and Independents as regards the way the offspring of Christians were regarded. The latter saw them as sharing the holy status of their parents, included in the covenant of grace, members of the church and entitled to baptism. The Baptist Confession, however, omits all reference to the covenant, children and parents in its statement on baptism which it allows only to 'those who do actually profess repentance towards God, faith in and obedience to our Lord Jesus Christ'.[43] Perhaps they saw election as so entwined with the covenant, Christian parenthood and baptism that they thought omitting the word 'election' would help them make the point.

But it of course raised the question as to the status of Baptists' children, who could not be given the assurance of belonging to the covenant, or of receiving a holy status from their parents signed and sealed in baptism. What happened if their children died? What comfort could be given to Baptist parents? Their answer was unequivocal and unqualified, going far beyond Westminster or even Dort. However, it is necessary to make the slight reservation that in the England of 300 years ago these words were addressed to those who received the Confession, to believers and church members, so that 'infants' means 'your infants' rather than 'all infants'.

Be that as it may, C. H. Spurgeon, who was totally committed to the Confession, had no hesitation in dogmatically asserting the salvation of all dying in infancy. In a letter of 1869 he wrote:

'I have never at any time in my life said, believed or imagined that any infants under any circumstances would be cast into hell. I have always believed in the salvation of all infants ... I do not believe that on this earth there is a single professing Christian holding the damnation of infants; or if there be he must be insane or utterly ignorant of Christianity'.[44]

There seems no room here for qualifications or reservations, and similar views were expressed from time to time in his preaching. On 29 September 1861, in a sermon preached in the Metropolitan Tabernacle and later published in Volume 7, he comforted bereaved parents with the words: 'Do you know what sorrows your little one has escaped? You have had enough yourself. It was born of woman; it might have been full of trouble as you are. It has escaped those sorrows; do you lament that?'

Nor was Spurgeon uttering some new strange doctrine. It appears that this view had become generally held by this time, not only among Arminians but also Calvinists and not only among Baptists but also Paedo-baptists. The Eclectic Society, which included such as John Newton and Thomas Scott, at a meeting in 1802 was unanimous on this point. Newton also gave this as his opinion in private correspondence.

The Presbyterian Church of the U.S.A., finding the statement in the Westminster Confession (X. 3) equivocal, clarified its position in 1903 thus: 'It is not regarded as teaching that any who die in infancy are lost. We believe that all dying in infancy are included in the election of grace, and are regenerated and saved by Christ through the Spirit who works when and where and how he pleases'.[45]

Other Reformed theologians of that period quoted by Hendriksen endorse this. Charles Hodge: 'All who die in infancy are saved. This is inferred from what the Bible teaches of the analogy between Adam and Christ (Rom. 5:18,19) ... The Scriptures nowhere exclude any class of infants, baptised or unbaptised, born in Christian or heathen lands, of believing or unbelieving parents, from the benefits of redemption in Christ.'

B. B. Warfield: 'Their destiny is determined irrespective of their choice, by an unconditional decree of God, suspended for its execution on no act of their own; and their salvation is wrought by an unconditional application of the grace of Christ to their souls, through the immediate and irresistible operation of the Holy Spirit prior to and apart from any action of their own proper wills ... This is but to say they are unconditionally predestinated to salvation from the foundation of the world.'

L. Boettner: 'Most Calvinistic theologians have held that those who die in infancy are saved ... Certainly there is nothing in the Calvinistic system which would prevent us from believing this; and until it is proven that God could not predestinate to eternal life all those whom he is pleased to call in infancy we may be permitted to hold this view'.[46]

All this is not far away from the position of W. H. Griffith-Thomas referred to earlier that 'all children are included in the great atoning sacrifice'.

3. The destiny of those dying in infancy is not revealed

Those who expressed the previous view did so as citizens of 'Christian nations' and at times when Christianity was the majority faith. Our century has seen a great decline from this faith among our own people accompanied by an influx of people from all over the world who have barely heard of Christianity and for the most part adhere to other faiths. To say 'all dying in infancy are saved', therefore, commits us to saying the children of atheists are saved, along with those of Muslims, Hindus and Buddhists, not to speak of cultists and occultists. This would even be the case where a Christian salvation was the last thing the parents wanted for their dead offspring.

It may be that this whole change of atmosphere has made recent theologians more hesitant in declaring the salvation of all dying infants. Some have tended to return to the doctrine of Dort, such as H. Bavinck: 'The children of the covenant, baptised or unbaptised, when they die enter heaven; with respect to the destiny of others, so little has been revealed to us that the best thing we can do is to refrain from any positive judgement' (*Gereformeede Dogmatiek IV.* p. 711).[46] Likewise L. Berkhof: 'There is no Scripture evidence on which we can base the hope that ... Gentile children that have not yet come to years of discretion will be saved' (*Systematic Theology* pp. 638, 693).[46]

Nor is this hesitation only expressed by Paedo-baptists. From the Baptist side David Kingdon wrote in *Children of Abraham*: 'It seems to me that if Spurgeon, Hodge and Boettner do not intentionally go beyond Scripture they certainly take the barest hints and press them so much that they become the assertion of this doctrine of infant salvation. But nowhere in Scripture, as far as I can see, is there express warrant for this belief. This is not to say that God cannot save all children dying in infancy, nor to say that he does not, it is simply to record the fact that he has not chosen to tell us whether he has or not ... My own position is that in the matter of infant salvation one can only adopt an attitude of reverent and hopeful agnosticism. One dare not add to Scripture, but neither must one make the deduction from Scripture that God cannot or will not save all children dying in infancy. The salvation of all children dying in infancy is not asserted in Scripture, nor is the condemnation of such children asserted. The mercy of God is free and large. That we know'.[47]

We do indeed have to admit that the Scriptures advanced in support of the universal salvation of dying infants are far from conclusive. The Westminster Confession cites Luke 18:15 ('suffer the children ...'), Acts 2:38f ('the promise is to you and your children'), John 3:3,5 ('except a man be born again ...'), 1 John 5:12 ('he that hath the Son hath life') and Romans 8:9 ('if the Spirit of God dwell in you ...'). The last three passages make no reference to children. In the Acts passage the promise about children is qualified by 'all whom the Lord our God will call'. About the passage in Luke (found also in Matt. 19:13-15; Mark 10:13-16) two things may be said: i) the children he blesses either come to or are brought to him, which obviously restricts their application to believers; ii) the meaning of 'of such is the kingdom' ('the kingdom belongs to such', N.I.V.) does not mean it belongs to them as children, but to those who approach him like children. Jesus went on to say 'anyone who will not receive the kingdom of God like a little child will never enter it' (Luke 18:17). The children who came or were brought to him were examples of how to come — simply, trustfully, dependently, and expectantly.[48]

A verse not yet mentioned but which is often appealed to is 2 Samuel 12:23. Before the death of his and Bathsheba's child, David had spent several nights fasting and laying on the ground in his room praying. As soon as the child died he washed and changed and worshipped in the Lord's house. Asked to explain his behaviour he said, 'While the child was still alive I fasted and wept. I thought, "Who knows? The Lord may be gracious to me and let the child live." But now he is dead why should I fast? Can I bring him back again? **I will go to him, but he will not return to me.**'

It is said that David believed his child was in heaven whither he himself was bound. However, the whole matter of life after death was a great unknown to the Old Testament saints. The most frequent word is '*Sheol*'. David himself described this in Psalm 6:5: 'No one remembers you (God) when he is dead. Who praises you from his grave (*Sheol*)?' Here is none of the conscious glad worshipping of departed believers we find in Revelation. Job actually looked forward to being in this state, and described it as the experience of the still-born child (3:11-19)! 'Heaven(s)' in the Old Testament means 'everywhere that is not "earth"', especially the abode of God, but not spoken of as the destiny of his people. It was not appealed to as a means of comforting the dying or bereaved.

It is plain that David is not here concerned about the child's eternal destination, but is simply occupied with whether the child lived or died. This was the burden of his prayer. When God took the child, David showed he accepted this. He was content, knowing that he couldn't bring him back, however much he fasted and prayed. The road between life and death is one-way. The child could not come back down it, but David himself would take it and follow him. 'I will go to him' means 'I too will die and go to Sheol'; 'he will not return to me' means 'he will not come back to life'. To read more into it is to go beyond what he had in mind. This is not to rob the words of their value for the bereaved. Parents suffer endless agonies over their lost children (and others) because they will not let them go. If they follow David and accept that they have gone, they experience great liberation, as David did.

Nor is it altogether surprising that we lack scriptural data on such a matter as the destiny of ignorant babes. The Bible is addressed to those who can hear and understand language and receive ideas. It calls for a hearing, followed by understanding and response. Those who cannot do these things are not addressed by the Bible. It is not a book of philosophy in which all the questions we could ever ask are discussed and answered. It is 'sufficient' in the sense that it tells all we **need** to know, not all we would **like** to know. It does not hypothesise about matters which are one remove or more away from ourselves. It leaves many of our questions unanswered. For example it does not answer our question 'Why do the righteous suffer and the wicked get off?' Or as we might put it, 'Why has this happened to me (him, her, them)? What have I (he, etc) done to deserve this?' It was with such questions that Job, Asaph (Ps. 73) and Habakkuk wrestled.

In such matters we have to fall back on the knowledge we have. We do not know what God does with our dead little ones, but we do know something far better, something which is the key to all conundrums — **what sort of God he is**. This he has shown us. He is a God altogether to be trusted — just, wise and loving. He will always and only do what is best. This is no doubt why, when such as C. H. Spurgeon proclaimed his view, he did not waste time over inconclusive texts, but declared the character of God. What sort of God is he? The sort that snatches babies from their mother's bosom and punishes them in hell? To Spurgeon such a God is unthinkable, certainly not the Father of our suffering Saviour.

There is therefore good hope for our children, and any children, who die. All will be well with them. God will do the best for them. What that best is we are not told. They don't fit the picture of heaven as we have it, where worship is consciously and intelligently offered by those who came to know Christ here. But no doubt heaven is much greater than the rather sketchy picture we have of it. Nor do we have to fall back on the Roman '*limbus infantum*'. God will give them something better than that!

What is even more certain is that we cannot fit them into hell as we know it. Hell is a place of punishment for sinners. What sin have they committed? Jesus described it as a place of burning shame and endless remorse ('where their worm does not die and the fire is not quenched', Mark 9:48). What have they to be ashamed of or remorseful about? A former writer expressed it thus: 'Infants are not capable of remorse or anguish of conscience. There is reason to believe this will be the chief feature of future punishment ... But as infants commit no actual sin, so there is no consciousness of it: nor can it be conveyed to them by any imputed guilt from Adam. Infants are not capable of a sense of divine dereliction ... as they have acquired no ideas of a God, a creature, a law, obedience and disobedience, sin and duty, the favour and anger of God, they could not acquire these but by the impression of God on their minds, and it is not to be imagined that God would give them these ideas purposely to punish them'.[49]

The only thing that could be held against them is their 'imputed guilt'. Is it beyond the wisdom and power of God to be able to deal with that? Before Jesus came there seemed no way of removing it from any of us: 'How shall a man be just with God?' was Job's unanswered question. But God found one. Indeed he had prepared it before ever the need arose. The incarnation and atonement of his Son, which none expected nor could have entered into the mind of man, came to fill the bill.

Whether he has included dying infants in that atonement, as some say, or has another way of solving the problem, he hasn't told us. But there is every hope for saying he has solved it. We live by faith, by trusting God, not only in the light of the green pasture, but in the darkness of the valley of the shadow of death. God does not have to tell us all the answers. Perhaps we would not be able to understand or receive them if he did. Or perhaps we just don't need to know. To trust is enough. Because of what we know of God we can be quite sure he has made provision for our children who leave us while in their state of ignorance and 'moral irresponsibility'. 'Imputed guilt' may present a problem to us but 'his ways are higher than ours' (Isa. 55:9). Who can have anything but hope for those two-year-olds and under whom Herod slaughtered in his search for the infant Jesus (Matt. 2:16)?

D. DIVINE PROTECTION

That it is right to think positively of the eternal destiny of children prior to their attaining years of discretion is confirmed when we look at the special care and protection God promises them. This does not apply only to the very young, nor just to children, but to all who are particularly vulnerable and defenceless. But none is more so than the infant.

1. *The Bible shows that God recognises and takes note of this weak position.* For example, he admits that in an attack of wild beasts the children will come off worst.[50] In a severe famine it will be the children who are the first victims of the outbreak of cannibalism.[51] We find even Jacob, not the most Godlike of the patriarchs, ensuring the utmost protection for the children as he set out to meet Esau and his 400 men.[52] They are very susceptible to false teaching and worship, as Jeremiah said, 'Even their children remember their altars and Asherah poles beside the spreading trees and on the high hills' (Jer. 17:2)

2. ***The Bible goes further to declare that God takes their part against their oppressors.*** If children generally are vulnerable then the fatherless are so most of all. But God will hear them when no one else does.[53] He takes personal charge of them.[54] So he is called 'a father to the fatherless' (Ps. 68:5), the one in whom 'the fatherless find compassion' (Hos. 14:3). Moreover he is angry with those who exploit or refuse them aid.[55] And he absolutely forbids the child sacrifice practised by some nations.[56]

3. ***This means so much to God that he has written it into his law***, so that those who call themselves his people will do as he does: i) they are to share their provisions with them and see they are fed;[57] ii) they are to ensure justice is done to them.[58] In these ways all will have a share in the common good.[59]

4. ***The same spirit is to be shown by Christians under the gospel.*** James wrote that 'Religion that God our Father accepts ... is this: to look after orphans and widows in their distress' (Jas. 1:27). In fact Jesus' teaching goes well beyond that of the Old Testament. In Matthew 18, when asked about greatness in his kingdom Jesus' reply was to point them to a little child and tell them they must all become like it to have a place in his kingdom at all. But the child is not only an example, he is a real human being, important to Christ. He identified himself with them, saying that the way a child was treated was the way he was treated. So a child must be 'welcomed' (v. 6), which was a rebuke to those, even his disciples, who wanted to keep them away.[60] He however accepted them and their faith — something he did not always do.[61]

He went on to warn them of the seriousness of causing them to sin in verses 7-9. Even to 'despise' them was forbidden. Lenski says this means 'to think down on, as though these little ones could be disregarded, as though they amounted to little or nothing'. To look down on young children was the common attitude of Jews, just as it was to look down on women and Gentiles. Jesus revolutionised the whole position of these classes.

5. Perhaps the high point of his view lies in ***the reason Jesus gives as to why they should not be despised***: 'For I tell you that their angels in heaven always see the face of my Father in heaven' (Matt. 18:10). When Jesus wanted to lay something on the line he used

phrases like 'I tell you'. As Plummer says, 'That shows how precious each one of them is in God's sight and what God values so highly men must not despise'.[62]

The Jews were familiar with the idea of the guardianship of angels over the people of God and frequently sang of it.[63] They would certainly have agreed with the apostle who wrote: 'Are not all angels ministering spirits sent to serve those who will inherit salvation?' (Heb. 1:14). That quotation shows this ministry was to continue under the gospel. Peter and other apostles were to experience it in literal and dramatic fashion when persecuted and imprisoned.[64] Jesus himself had benefited from it as a young child;[65] also when he was oppressed by Satan at the outset of his ministry.[66] He was later to experience it in his great weakness when struggling with his flesh in Gethsemane.[67]

It is Jesus alone who specifically mentions children in connection with angelic ministry in Matthew 18:10, quoted above. Clearly he is not going to the other extreme and saying that children are singled out for special treatment. This ministry is for all believers; and it is of believers, the childlike, he is speaking here. He says that children benefit from it as much as, if not more than, other believers. It is unlikely that Jesus was endorsing the view that each believer has a personal angel. This was held by some Jews, as the book of Tobit shows, a view shared, it appears, by those Christians who heard that Peter was out of prison and standing at their door, who said, 'It must be his angel' (Acts 12:15). 'Their angels' means that not one angel but the whole angelic band was on hand to help. As Matthew Henry wrote: 'Some have imagined that every particular saint has a guardian angel; but why should we suppose this when we are sure that every particular saint, when there is occasion, has a guard of angels?'.[68]

The point is that whereas in the Old Testament God cared for children through the ministry of adults, the New Testament shows us a double ministry — that of his believing people on earth and his angels in heaven. Lenski has written: 'Here Jesus mentions two classes of ministrants for each of these little ones: the disciples who are still on earth and these heavenly angels; the disciples who have not yet attained perfection and the *"visio Dei"*, and the angels who always see the countenance of the Father. God appoints both classes of ministrants to carry out his gracious will regarding each of these little ones'.[69]

Surely this is a source of peace for parents who worry excessively over their infant children. They are not alone in the care they feel. God can also protect them from dangers over which parents have no power, especially in the moral and spiritual realm. True as it is that we are in a state of sin from the womb,[70] this is not the sum total of the truth about us. We do not have to jump to conclusions, such as: 'The Bible says my child can do nothing but wickedness and God will have nothing to do with it because of the Adamic curse'; or 'If it dies before I can explain the gospel and bring it to repentance and faith it will go to hell.' We must examine *all* the biblical data on children before we draw our conclusions. Especially we must be sure that what we conclude must be in keeping with the character of God, the all-just, all-wise, all-loving, all-powerful.

References

Section II: Part I, A

1   *Children of the King*, p. 19
2   Op. cit. p. 110
3   Quoted in *Realities of Childhood*, p. 110
4   *Ibid.* p.111
5   *Principles of Theology*, p. 378
6   Inchley: *Realities of Childhood*, p. 110
7   Buckland: *Children and God*, p. 17
8   *Ibid.* p. 29
9   *Ibid.* pp. 29-30
10 *Ibid.* p. 42
11 *Ibid.* p. 43
12 *Ibid.* p. 45
13 Quoted in Buckland: *Children of the King*, p. 15
14 *Ibid.* p. 15
15 *Children and God*, p. 31
16 Calvin: *First Corinthians*, Oliver & Boyd 1960, p. 149
17 *Institutes II.* i.7
18 Marcel: *Biblical Doctrine of Infant Baptism*, pp. 196-7
19 J. Murray: *Christian Baptism*, p. 68
20 Commentary on 1 Corinthians, p. 165
21 *Children of Abraham*, p. 93
22 *Children and God*, p. 27
23 *Ibid.* p. 42
24 *Ibid.* pp. 29-30
25 Rom. 4:24
26 Gen. 2:17; 3:19
27 Rom. 6:23

Section II: Part I, B

28 Inchley, op. cit. p.111
29 Pridmore: *New Testament Theology of Childhood*, p. 49
30 *Ibid.* p. 46
31 Exod. 34:7; Deut. 5:9; 24:16
32 2 Kings 14:5f
33 Exod. 20:12
34 Ps. 37:26, 28, 37f
35 Jer. 31:31-34
36 Rom. 1:18-32
37 Buckland: *Children of the King*, p. 68
38 Ps. 51:5

Section II: Part I, C

39 *Letters of Samuel Rutherford.* Bonar Edition, Letter 238
40 Articles of the Synod of Dort I.17
41 Westminster Confession of Faith X.3
42 Baptist Confession of Faith, 1689, ch. 10.
43 *Ibid.* ch. 29
44 Quoted by Gary Brady: 'Infant Salvation', in *Foundations* No:30 (British Evangelical Council)
45 Quoted in Hendriksen: *Bible and the Life Hereafter*, p. 101
46 *Ibid.* p. 102
47 Op. cit. pp. 97-8
48 There will be an extended discussion on this passage in pp. 72-76
49 J. H. Pratt: *The thought of the Evangelical leaders*, p. 260

Section II: Part I, D

50 Lev. 26:22
51 Deut. 28:54-57
52 Gen. 32:11; 33:13
53 Exod. 22:22-26
54 Deut. 10:18; Ps. 10:14,18
55 Isa. 1:23
56 Lev. 18:21
57 Deut. 24:19-21
58 Deut. 24:17; 27:19; Ps. 82:3f; Isa. 1:17
59 Deut. 14:29; 16:11,14
60 Matt. 19:13
61 John 2:23-25
62 A. Plummer: *Exegetical Commentary on Matthew*, p. 251
63 Ps. 34:7; 91:11
64 Acts 5:19; 12:11
65 Matt. 1:20; 2:13,19
66 Matt. 4:11
67 Luke 22:43
68 M. Henry: *Exposition of Old and New Testaments*, in. loc.
69 R. C.H. Lenski: *Interpretation of Matthew's Gospel*, p. 692
70 Ps. 51:5

Part II:
The child's salvation

In this chapter we are thinking of children as they move out of that
state of 'moral irresponsibility' (Inchley) and 'spiritual helplessness' (Buckland) into one in which understanding is dawning and
with it, the beginnings of response. Although the transition from
night to day is slow and gradual, it is real. Words begin to mean
something as opposed just to tones of voice and body language.
Ideas are perceived and understood so that some sort of response is
produced.

As responsiveness develops so does responsibility. This affects
matters already discussed: sin, moral responsibility and relationship
to God. The special arrangements God has for the oblivious are
being left behind and the child is coming into that stage of life to
which the statements and invitations of Scripture are addressed —
the stage of 'intelligence'. We can now think of children in relation
to the Bible's call to obey God, repent of sin, believe the gospel and
thus become saved. What does the Bible teach about children and
salvation? Do they respond consciously and deliberately to the
gospel like adults? These are the questions we must now address.

A. A CHILD'S NEED OF SALVATION

Not everyone agrees that children need to make a conscious response to the call to salvation. Some do not think calls to repent and
believe are appropriate. Children, even those out of the baby stage,
do not need an evangelistic challenge; they come into another
category. On this question we therefore need to take account of a
number of different views.

1. The view that children have a 'natural faith'

Walter H. Werner wrote: 'All children are born with a natural faith. Children readily believe almost everything they hear. This experience carries over into every experience, including the area of salvation'.[1] This view lies behind the position adopted by John Inchley that children do not need to experience 'conversion' in the same way as adults: 'Many children, especially those brought up in an atmosphere of Christian teaching at home or in the church, will have no need for "conversion" in the exact meaning of the word as they make their personal response to the Saviour'.[2]

He cites a bishop who began his address to a Scripture Union rally by saying, 'The first thing I have to tell you is that I have never been converted', and who spoke of remembering that he had never made a negative response to Christ from his boyhood.[2] He also quotes Campbell Morgan: 'When the necessity came for my personal choosing, so did I recognise the claims of Christ's love that, without revulsion and hardly knowing when, I yielded to him my allegiance and my love, devoting spirit, soul and body to his sweet will and glad service'.[3] Finally Inchley alludes to his own experience: 'This was also the pattern of my own response when as a boy of seven I put my trust in the Lord Jesus for myself. There was no experience of conversion in the proper Bible meaning of the word, for I could not remember the time when I had not loved him'.[2]

He explains this by claiming that children already have the qualities that constitute faith: 'gentleness, trust, friendliness, tolerance, liveliness, courage, generosity, adaptability, wonder and humanness ... Wise parents will use this intrinsic trust in themselves to the greater experience of trusting God as a heavenly Father'.[4] This is similar to Buckland's view that in ministering to children the important word is 'nurture', a word which applies not only to growth towards maturity but 'includes the idea of **initiating** the children of Christian parents into an understanding of their potential Christian heritage'.[5] Realising that in the opinion of many 'this teaching cuts the nerve of evangelism among children', he suggests that the two ideas are not incompatible: 'Are education and evangelism really two completely different entities? Is it not possible to hold that all children should be nurtured within the framework of evangelistic urgency?'.[5] Unfortunately he does not develop this view, merely concluding, 'The relationship between teaching, nurture and evangelism needs more attention'.[5]

It would be easy to overreact against this view. That many ongoing Christians cannot remember a D-day in their lives or even a phase of change is something we must accept. It is not just that time has erased it from the memory, for many important childhood experiences remain in our thoughts until our last day. It is that the experience was not such a change as to constitute a crisis. This does not, however, mean that no change took place. Rather it means that at a time when thinking had not hardened, habits were unformed and character undeveloped, the experience was not one of **change** so much as **growth**.

But it does not mean that children do not need to be saved or to come to salvation by a conscious response. This is a matter of theology rather than experience. We have already observed the tendency in these writers to allow experience to modify theology. In any case, a careful reading of these experiences reveals that they themselves admit that 'a personal response to the Saviour' is involved. Campbell Morgan spoke of 'recognising the claims of Christ' and 'yielding allegiance to him'. John Inchley said of himself, 'I put my trust in the Lord' and he was prepared to use the word 'conversion', though not 'in the proper Bible meaning' or in the same sense as adults.[2]

What then of the 'natural faith' that is claimed for children? Again, an overreaction would be the easiest response. But what Inchley said of children is true — the qualities he mentions **are** the qualities of children. Children are avid to learn — not only to acquire knowledge but to respond practically and learn to do things for themselves. This includes the religious realm where they are confronted with it. They will be interested to know what it teaches and inasfar as it calls on them to act, they will be quick to carry out its demands. This, however, while it can in a sense be called 'faith', is not necessarily **saving** faith. There are occasions in the ministry of Jesus where people responded positively both to his teaching and challenge, and are even said to 'believe', yet they did not become disciples, those to whom the word 'saved' could be applied.[6] Similarly a child's 'natural faith', by which it appears to accept the truth presented and to act upon it, is not necessarily saving faith.

2. The view that children as such are 'in the kingdom'

In the discussion on children and sin in the previous chapter, we noted that some doubted whether it was right to speak of children as 'sinners' since Jesus spoke of them as 'belonging to his kingdom'. If this is the case they will not need to make a conscious response to the offer of salvation. This is deduced from the words of Jesus 'of such is the kingdom of heaven' (AV) or 'the kingdom of heaven belongs to such as these' (NIV) in Matthew 19:14, Mark 10:14, Luke 18:16. This would seem to be the appropriate place to examine these words more closely.

The great commentators are divided over the precise reference of the words 'as such' (Greek *toiouton*).

a. There are those who seem to apply it to the children of believers **as children**, such as Matthew Henry: 'The children of believing parents belong to the kingdom of heaven and are members of the visible church. Of such, not only in disposition and affection ... but in age, is the kingdom ...' Matthew Poole would seem to take the same line, in view of his connecting of the words with infant baptism.

b. Others apply it not to children as children but to those who are like children. Plummer points out that the word is *toiouton* not *touton*, that is, those **like** children: 'Not those particular children nor all children, but those who are childlike in character are possessors of the kingdom'. Geldenhuys takes the same line and quotes Jerome in support: 'It is not these children but those who are childlike in character, especially in humility and trustfulness, who are best fitted for the kingdom'. Lenski is even more definite: 'Not "of these", the ones now being brought, but "of such" ... the great class of beings to which babes as such belong ... They are model examples of the whole class. If we want to know the character of the class we must study children. It is their receptivity to which Jesus refers'.

c. Calvin saw a double reference, both to children as such and the childlike: 'Under this term he includes both little children and those who resemble them', but he does not specify whether the children referred to are only those of believers. Recent writers on the subject hold this view even more strongly and commit themselves to referring the words to children generally. J. S. Pridmore in an unpublished thesis, 'The New Testament theology of childhood', makes a thorough examination of *toiouton* which, according to the Greek Lexicon of Arndt and Gingrich can refer either to a 'definite individual' or a 'bearer of certain definite qualities'. He quotes some uses of this word where it is applied not to the bearers of certain qualities but to particular individuals:

Acts 22:22: 'Rid the earth of him' (*toiouton*); it is for the death of Paul himself not of people like him that they are crying out.

Romans 16:18: 'For such people (*toiouton*) are not serving the Lord Christ.' This refers to particular individuals who were a divisive influence in Rome.[7] This leads Pridmore to conclude that Mark 10:14 means that 'the kingdom of heaven belongs to children and those like them'.

Ron Buckland, influenced by such as Pridmore, says that Jesus is not only using children as a visual aid to challenge adults, but making a statement about all children: 'the kingdom of God belongs to them. Jesus seems to be doing two things at once. He challenges adults that they will never find a way into the kingdom unless they become childlike ... At the same time and on the basis of the adult challenge towards childlikeness Jesus teaches that children already belong to the Kingdom of God'.[8] He then proceeds to discuss this in relation to the various answers commonly given to the question of the status of children in relation to the kingdom. To him it means that children begin with God but will drift away unless they are 'nurtured' (in the case of the children of Christians) or 'evangelised' (in the case of the children of non-Christians). This shows how central to the whole matter of child nurture and child evangelism is this statement.

It cannot be denied that the words as they stand are ambiguous and that 'strict grammatical considerations cannot settle for us the width of reference intended'.[9] Other canons of interpretation have to be brought into the equation, the chief of which is context. Pridmore uses this canon in the case of the other instances of *toiouton* he quotes, but fails to let the context determine the matter in Mark 10:13-16. Having said in verse 14 that 'the kingdom of God belongs to such as these', Jesus immediately explains what he means by this in verse 15: 'anyone who will not receive the kingdom of God as a little child will never enter it'. '**As** a little child' cannot mean the same as '**when** a little child', which would say too much for any contributor to the discussion, for it would exclude all except children. It would mean that unless you come into the kingdom during childhood it will be too late! It must therefore mean 'in the way a little child receives it'. Vincent Taylor renders the words in this way and Pridmore agrees with him. Evidently there is something about the way children receive things which is an example to all who would receive the kingdom. Children who do receive the kingdom have no problem doing it in the right way, because there is something in childhood which fits them for it. This is to be emulated by others.

Pridmore admirably expresses what this spirit is: 'the capacity of a child to receive something as a gift is what Jesus had in mind ... the kingdom cannot be earned.' He quotes Cranfield: 'To receive the kingdom as a little child is to allow oneself to be given it'. This is Jesus' own exposition of his words 'of such is the kingdom' or 'the kingdom belongs to such as these'. By them he means that those who belong to the kingdom are those who receive it in the way children receive things, that is, in a state of helplessness and as a free gift. Children do not belong to it because they are children; anyone who emulates their receptivity can belong to it.

This interpretation is confirmed by several other considerations:

a. Jesus' action in verse 16 which, as Pridmore points out, is a fulfilment of Isaiah 40:11: 'he gathers the lambs in his arms and carries them close to his heart'. 'The lambs' are not children as such, but the weak and helpless, the kind of people for whom the Messiah came. This is similar to what Jesus said in John 21:15-16 to Peter: 'Feed my lambs ... take care of my sheep'. The lambs are the new entrants into the flock, still in their weak and helpless state, and the sheep are the more established and secure disciples. Those who come to him in helplessness he takes into his arms, be they children or adults.

b. In the previous chapter, Mark 9:33-41, we have other references to Jesus and children. Here Jesus and his disciples are in Peter's house in Capernaum where Jesus asks them to tell him about their argument over greatness in the kingdom, which had been occupying them along the road. Jesus settles the argument by stating that 'the greatest' are 'the very last and servant of all'. He then grabs one of the children of the house, possibly one of Peter's own, and uses him to exemplify the point. To become 'last and servant' is to become like a little child.

The status of children in that age was like that of servants — one of utter insignificance, very different from the regard in which they are held today. In the Roman Empire the children of the household were brought up with the slaves' children and supervised by slaves. [10] It is this same status we must accept for ourselves in order to join the kingdom. Possibly the 'Strange Exorcist' of the next few verses is an example of a child in the faith who is not to be refused because of his weak understanding (not realising who Jesus is) or his weak will (not resolute enough to come and join his band) verse 39. Then in verse 41 the disciples are told they will be served by others in the kingdom. This goes with verse 37 — those who welcome 'little children', such as the disciples were, welcome Jesus. The disciples were not children, but were like children.

c.   Another similar children passage is Matthew 18:1-10. Again the child is used as a lesson to the adult who would like to be in the kingdom. He must become like a little child, he must adopt a very insignificant, weak, helpless, receptive mind-set. This for an adult involves a 'change' (v. 3) and a self-humbling (v. 4). Jesus is not saying 'children are naturally humble' in the sense that they **feel** humble. This is far from the case! In their own eyes they are the centre of the universe! He is saying they are in a very humble and lowly **position**, whether they realise it or not. We must all come to this to get into the kingdom, which is exactly what Mark 10:14 is saying.

d.   The Lucan parallel to Mark 10 is 18:15-17. Luke uses a term which means 'tiny babies', those only just born. This further emphasises the point, for who is more helpless and weak than a tiny baby? All such a one can do is to receive, everything has to be given it, the milk is put into its mouth and it only has to suck and swallow. What a vivid picture of how we receive the kingdom! What a confirmation that Mark 10:14 describes the way we must all enter the kingdom!

There is therefore no ground for alleging that Jesus teaches that all children belong to the kingdom and have no need to be 'saved' and brought into it.

3. The view that children of believing parents are included in the covenant of grace

Reference has been made to this in discussing the subject of sin in relation to children. Although those who hold this view do not necessarily exclude children from the Adamic curse, it must make a difference to the way they assess their need of salvation and to the way they approach them. There will not be the same stress on calling them to repent and believe as there would be if they were seen as outside this gracious relationship and under sentence of death.

Louis Berkhof, in writing of the inclusion of believers' children in the covenant, admits that in their case the covenant is 'a legal relationship' rather than 'a communion of life'. Presumably this means they are born 'in Adam' with all that carries with it. 'Yet even in their case there must be reasonable assurance that the covenant will not remain a mere legal relationship ... but will in time become a living reality ... It carries with it the assurance based on the promises of God ... that saving faith will be wrought in their hearts. As long as the children of the covenant do not reveal the contrary, we shall have to proceed on the assumption that they are in possession of covenant life.' However, since there is no cast-iron guarantee 'that he will endow every last one of them with saving faith ... it is necessary to remind even children of the covenant constantly of the necessity of regeneration and conversion'.[11]

In spite of the disclaimer, clearly such children have a head start over others, and those who fail to make the short journey from the 'legal relationship' to the 'communion of life' are the exceptions. The biblical teaching from which this is deduced is not given at this point but is reserved for the later discussion on baptism, just as it is in Calvin and the Westminster Confession. Since, however, the basis of baptising infants is their inclusion in the covenant, we can take it that the Scriptures which teach the one teach the other.

Two of these Scriptures have already been referred to: the words of Jesus concerning children in Mark 10:13-16 and of Paul to the Corinthians in 1 Corinthians 7:14: 'your children are holy'. The former has just received a full discussion. In the case of the latter we saw that the most frequent explanation of the holiness of children was to connect it with the covenant. In the words of John Murray it is 'the holiness of connection and privilege ... that evinces the operation of the covenant'.[12] This is a very attractive idea, for who would not want to feel their children share with them in their special relationship with God? Unfortunately there is a flaw in the exegesis. Paul began by speaking of the unbelieving partner being 'sanctified' by the believer. This word is simply the verb of which 'holy' is the adjective. No commentator seems prepared to make it mean something different. Neither is any prepared to say that an unbelieving partner is included in the covenant through marriage to a believer. In their case, being of mature years, a personal response is required. In what way then can an unbeliever be thought of as 'holy'? Good hermeneutical principles would tell us that this must be determined by the subject and context.

The Corinthians' problem was whether a believer should continue to have marital relations with an unbelieving spouse. Would they be defiled by such contact? Should they refuse marital relations or even leave home? Do neither, says Paul; separate neither from bed nor board. Your marriage is not defiled in God's sight by relations with an unbeliever. If it were your children also would be affected. The term is used in a moral or ceremonial sense not a spiritual one. There is no reference here to covenant.

Another verse appealed to is Acts 2:39. The Jews, convicted of crucifying their Messiah, ask Peter, 'What shall we do?' to which Peter replies, 'Repent and be baptised every one of you for the forgiveness of your sins, and you will receive the gift of the Holy Spirit'. He encourages them with many words, beginning with 'the promise is for you and your children and for all who are far off — for all whom the Lord our God will call'. On this Calvin says 'that the benefit of the gospel belongs to them and their offspring by right of the covenant'.[13] There is however no mention here of the Abrahamic covenant. 'The promise' is clearly the promise of the Spirit, just specified in v. 38. It was in this way our Lord had spoken of him,[14] as Paul was to later in Ephesians 1:13. The original promise is found in Ezekiel 36:27 and Joel 2:28-32, which Peter had quoted fully to explain the phenomena which had drawn his hearers together on that occasion. Peter is saying: 'You can have not only your sins forgiven but a share in this gift God has bestowed on us'.

It is not Berkhof's 'legal relationship' which Peter is promising

to them and their children but his 'communion of life' — the life of
the Spirit. For although the **phenomena** of Pentecost would not be
universal the **essence** of the gift of the Spirit would be for all who
respond to 'the call'. In other words the blessings of the **new**
covenant were coming to pass. This was not a mere 'legal relationship' for the people of one race or generation, but 'life' for all races
throughout time. So Peter is not saying it is for the babies of his
hearers, which restricts it too much. He is saying, 'This promise is
not only for this generation of Jews, but succeeding ones too, in fact
it is for Gentiles as well, for whoever God will call'. The phrase 'you
and your children' recalls the self-imprecation of Matthew 27:25:
'his blood be on us and our children', which means 'on all generations of our race'. Peter is saying 'that curse can be lifted on
repentance and replaced by a blessing'. 'This indwelling presence
is promised to St Peter's hearers and the Jewish race, and further
even to the Gentiles'.[15] Hosea 2:4 shows that 'children' can sometimes mean later generations: 'I will not show my love to her
children', referring to the descendants of the present generations of
the people of Judah.

The beneficiaries of the promise are in the sovereign will and
choice of God, who no longer restricts himself to Jewish families
and is not bound to call the specific children of those who respond.
There is indeed an allusion to the Abrahamic covenant, that 'in you
(Abraham) all nations of the earth will be blessed' (Gen. 12:3). But
the bestowal of that blessing is taken out of the Abrahamic line or
any other line and now given sovereignly by the effectual call of
God. There is a danger of confusing the methods by which the two
covenants, old and new, operated. The old brought children to God
by parental instruction and discipline. The new brings them to him
by regeneration, which is not in the hands of the parents but works
through God's grace and power.

Appealing as is the idea of a covenant that extends automatically
to the children of believers, it does not fit the terms of the new
covenant. It is too limiting; it makes us look for church growth
primarily through the inclusion of our children, rather than outside
our families. Indeed covenant theologians tend to see believers'
children as making the largest contribution to the numerical increase
of the kingdom. It is also somewhat out of character with the
sovereign choice of God and his effectual working in whom he will,
indeed with the whole New Testament stress on his grace. The

perfect freedom of God to call or pass over is modified. Our children have no automatic claim on God's mercy. They stand in just as much need of grace as the children of unbelievers.

4. The view that children, like adults, require regeneration in order to be saved

'Since every child is born into the Adamic humanity, every child must, if it is to know salvation, be regenerated and transferred into the new humanity in Christ. Children no less than adults require to be regenerated'.[16] This view arises out of the theological position regarding children and sin discussed in the previous chapter, which holds that children are not and never were, from conception, exempt from the state of sin and death which the whole race inherits from Adam. The sin, guilt and condemnation of Adam is imputed to all his descendants irrespective of age. However, it is not merely a deduction from that teaching. It is supported by passages which bear directly on the subject under discussion.

a. **John 3:6**: 'Flesh gives birth to flesh, but the Spirit gives birth to spirit.' It was with these words that Jesus backed up his declaration to Nicodemus that unless and until he is 'born again ... of water and the Spirit' he will 'not see (or) enter the kingdom of God' (vv. 3,5). The proof of this follows in verse 6: normal human birth only produces 'flesh', the biblical meaning of which is 'sinful human nature' (Rom. 8:5-8), not mere physical organs. From one sinful human being comes another of the same ilk. There has to be another birth if a spiritual being is to appear, one born of another parent, a spiritual parent, the Spirit himself. 'If the meaning of the text is to be upheld it allows of no exceptions — to be born is to be born of the flesh and thus to be laid under the necessity of being born again in order to see (i.e. experience) the kingdom of God'.[16]

b. **1 Corinthians 15:50**: 'I declare to you, brothers, that flesh and blood cannot inherit the kingdom of God, nor does the perishable inherit the imperishable.' This comes towards the end of a passage which is an important one identical to Romans 5:12ff, for Paul has again set forth Christ and Adam as two representative heads: 'as in Adam all die, so in Christ all will be made alive' (v. 22). We reject the universalist interpretation of this verse which makes 'all' in both parts of the sentence apply to the whole human race irrespective of knowledge or response to the gospel, for this would make Paul disagree with himself. Instead, we take it to mean, 'all in Adam die, all in Christ will be made alive'. The teaching is developed in verses 45-49, but basically he is saying what he said in Romans 5:12-14, that the nature of Adam is imputed to all his descendants, along with the resulting condemnation to death. This even applies to those ignorant of the law who have not consciously disobeyed.

In this passage, as in John 3, 'the kingdom' is brought into the equation. The kingdom, which some claim as the birthright of some or all children, apparently requires a transforming work. It requires the regeneration of which Jesus spoke in John 3, plus the glorification by resurrection of which Paul speaks here. It is clear that those who will be resurrected to a glorious body are those who die 'in Christ' (v. 22), those 'who belong to him' (v. 23), those who are spoken of as having 'faith' (v. 14) by which they are 'saved' (v. 2). The chapter makes a clear distinction between them and others: 'if only in this life we have hope in Christ we are to be pitied more than all men' (v. 19). 'We' are those who are in the kingdom by the new birth now and will be resurrected into the kingdom's consummation at his coming again (v. 24).

'It is hard to see that Paul's language in 1 Corinthians 15 admits of the exception of children. Nowhere does he hint that his meaning is to be restricted to responsible adults. Children do not become depraved in Adam when they assume responsibility. Since they are born in Adam they are depraved by nature from the very beginning of their existence. If so they must needs be regenerated by the sovereign power of our gracious God'.[17]

This view has to be set against the others discussed. If it is the biblical position then it rules out the view that children have a **'natural faith'** which dispenses with the need for a radical inward renewal. It is clearly not consistent with the view that children are **already in the kingdom**, because they too need another birth since their physical birth has not brought them into it. Nor are **children of believers** exempt from it. In fact the covenant theologians themselves concede this point — the holy status or 'legal relationship' does not mean they do not need regeneration, simply that they have a more specific promise of it.

We must not, however, overreact and treat these other views as utter rubbish. All have hit upon important truths. It is true that children are more likely to take things on trust than adults and this greatly facilitates the work of encouraging them to saving faith, although it does not in itself constitute saving faith or guarantee it. It is also true that Jesus himself made the state of childhood in some way a model of the way we must all enter the kingdom, though not going so far as to admit children by the door of human birth only, for this would mean they could choose to be turned out of it. Finally, there is no question that believers' children are in a different position from those of others because of their access to the **means** of regeneration which their parents have in their hands, whereas others must have outside witnesses to bring them the means. How all this affects the way they come into the kingdom has yet to be discussed. But we must take account of the various ways in which children occupy a special position as well as the way they are in the same position as the rest of us. We must not give a new meaning to the phrase 'throwing out the baby with the bath water'! These views are not to be poured down the drain like dirty bath water.

Our children do need regenerating if they are to be members of the kingdom. Like the rest of us they are outside it by nature and like the rest of us there is only one way in for them — the new birth. Moreover, they need it just as urgently as anyone else. For that state called 'flesh' is not a merely neutral physical condition. The word has moral and spiritual overtones. It means 'sinful nature', a nature to which Adam's sin has been charged. Nor is that just a formality. It is alive and will quickly work in a child to bring forth 'the works of the flesh', acts of sin. The more quickly a child's nature is changed by regeneration, the better.

B. A CHILD'S CAPABILITY OF CONVERSION

The doorway from the Adamic state and curse into the kingdom where salvation is enjoyed is regeneration. What is it? How is it experienced? What are its marks and fruits? Regeneration is what Jesus referred to in John 3 as the new birth. It is a work of God's power in our sinful human nature, by which we are brought from spiritual death to life and thus 'born again' into the kingdom of Christ. It leads to conversion, which is a turning from our own ways — our self-love, self-confidence, self-indulgence — to trust Christ alone and yield ourselves to him as Saviour and Lord. Those who experience it become aware that they are away from God and yet that he is drawing them to him. They come to see that he gave his Son

to suffer the punishment of their sins and thankfully receive his offer
of pardon in Christ. Such are 'born of the Holy Spirit' and know it.

The question is whether children are capable of this kind of
response. It does involve some understanding in the mind, some
feeling in the soul and response of the will. Are children capable of
these? Ron Buckland has expressed the view that they are 'spiritually helpless', proved by the fact that they had to be **brought** to Jesus
for his blessing.[18] They cannot be regarded or treated as individuals
but 'must be seen as family-related' so that 'the responsibility of
children is primarily one of obedience to parents'.[19]

There is no question that he has described a stage in the life of
every child. But it is also true that it soon begins to be left behind.
The first sign of this is when the child begins to understand words.
As this develops it gives birth to an understanding of the ideas
behind the words. He begins to have his own thoughts and is
becoming an individual distinct from the parent. He continues to
respond primarily to the parent but as thought-processes develop
and he learns to frame them into words, he becomes capable of
responding to these ideas. If the words and ideas fed to him include
God, sin and Jesus Christ he will slowly become capable of
responding to these. He will be able to believe that God is there
although unseen. He will have difficulty understanding **how** this can
be, but don't we all? Even when we develop philosophical explana-
tions and stop coming up with childlike notions about treading on
God or bumping into him, we don't necessarily understand these
notions. It takes time to believe what can't be visualised or even
imagined.

Similarly he will gradually come to see that naughtiness and
disobedience in the eyes of the parent constitute something more
serious in the eyes of this unseen God who is there. If at the same
time the person of Jesus is introduced to him and stories told of his
life and death, it will become possible for him to relate Jesus both
to God and his sin. He will be in the process of understanding the
way of salvation and deciding whether he wants it.

The Bible has astonishing statements about the relationship
between some children and God right from the womb. Rebekah was
told of the destiny of her twin sons before they were born, that 'the
older will serve the younger' (Gen. 25:23), which Paul uses to affirm
'God's purpose in election' (Rom. 9:11f). God told Jeremiah that he
had chosen him before birth.[20] Paul's claim for himself was that

'God ... set me apart from birth' (Gal. 1:15). Then there were children whose births were announced before the pregnancies of their mothers: Isaac, Samson, the Shunamite woman's son and John the Baptist.[21] Paul and Jeremiah of course had no knowledge of God's plans for them until they became men and were personally called by God. Yet with hindsight we can see God preparing these men from their childhood days. Of John the Baptist it was said he would be 'filled with the Holy Spirit even from birth' (Luke 1:15).

Samuel, although not the subject of statements like those above, was nevertheless born as a direct result of prayer, including the prayer of Eli the judge, which might almost amount to a prophecy, especially in view of the name given the child, 'heard of God'.[22] He was, upon weaning, dedicated to the Lord with a prayer which is virtually a prophecy,[23] and from that time went to work in the Tabernacle with Eli, who was priest as well as judge. He learned from an early age to distinguish the voice of God from that of Eli.[24] This was the occasion when he too was made a prophet, for 1 Samuel 3:7 must mean that 'the word of the Lord was revealed to him' so that he would proclaim it. The same expression is used in 1 Samuel 3:1: 'the word of the Lord was rare' and is connected with 'visions', which was the way the word was revealed to a prophet. Samuel is immediately given a prophetic word,[25] which he proceeds to declare to Eli. This first task as a prophet is followed over succeeding years by a regular ministry.[26]

Although these are rare instances, they indicate that children must be constitutionally **capable** of knowing God and responding to him and his word. We have also the words of David, 'from the lips of infants you have ordained praise' (Ps. 8:2). These words are quoted by Jesus to justify the acclamation given him by children on his entry into Jerusalem.[27] This could be a sign that what was the exception under the old covenant would become the norm under the new. Peter declared that the phenomena of Pentecost fulfilled Joel's prophecy that the Spirit which had been on prophets and special people would now become more widespread.[28] This would include 'sons and daughters' although nothing is said about their ages. However, Jesus spoke of marks of the Spirit's work that were appearing in children as they came to him. He spoke of them 'humbling themselves' (Matt. 18:4) and 'being caused to sin' (v. 6). If a child is capable of being caused to sin he is capable of knowing this and repenting. If he can 'humble himself' he can believe in Christ.

We are encouraged to believe in the potentiality of children in the intellectual, moral and spiritual realms by some of our forefathers. George Muller said: 'As far as my experience goes, it appears to me that believers generally have expected far too little present fruit upon their labours among children'. In 1866 Spurgeon addressed a conference on 'The Importance of Seeking the Conversion of the Young' in the course of which he remarked: 'No part of our population is of equal importance with the juvenile portion of it and I believe that among none beside will the same amount of earnest, prayerful, loving labour meet with a larger or even an equal measure of success'.[29]

In his famous 1864 sermon 'Children brought to Christ not to the Font', Spurgeon remarked: 'I do love to think that the gospel is suitable to little children. There are boys and girls in many of our Sabbath-school classes down below stairs who are as truly converted to God as any of us ... But a minister who preaches as though he never wanted to bring children to Christ, and shoots right over the little ones' heads, I do think Jesus is displeased with him.

'Then there are others who doubt whether children ever will be converted. They do not look upon it as a thing likely to happen, and whenever they hear of a believing child, they hold up their hands at the prodigy and say, "What a wonder of grace!" It ought to be ... as common a thing for children to be converted as for grown-up people to be brought to Christ. Others begin to doubt the truth of juvenile conversions. They say, "They are very young, can they understand the gospel? Is it not merely an infantile emotion, a mere profession?" My brethren, you have no more right to suspect the sincerity of the young than to mistrust the grey-headed; you ought to receive them with the same open-breasted confidence with which you receive others when they profess to have found the Saviour.'

Abraham Kuyper wrote: 'Provided family and other environment do not from the first choke the seed of religion in a child, the child mind is normally religious. Not by an outward show but by receptivity of holy impressions and by a hushed reverence before the Eternal Being. To teach a child to pray, if done under pious guidance and not mechanically, is a beautiful and tender joy ... Even when the child cannot yet read ... he stands instinctively in fellowship with the world of hidden things'.[30]

Statistical surveys indicate that at least as many date their arrival at personal faith to an age below twelve as those who date it afterwards. No doubt this is because the suitability of childhood for this outweighs its unsuitability. The literalism of children and their difficulties over abstracts create problems, but over against this must be set the advantages. It was no doubt these that were in the mind of Christ when he welcomed the children and took them in his arms, to the horror of the bystanders who would never have seen such behaviour from a rabbi. In Judaism it was not a case of 'children should be seen and not heard' — they should not even be seen. Then Jesus became more vile and told them they must change their whole attitude and become like the children themselves or they would be left out of the kingdom when the children were admitted.[31]

What is it about children that made Jesus say such things? It was certainly not that he saw them as innocent. We have already established that children are part of fallen humanity and need the saving grace of Christ just as much as adults. Once arrived at the age of responsibility they are called upon to repent and believe. But with their lack of years and inexperience of the world children will be **less steeped in sin** and therefore less hardened against the demand for repentance. They have not yet built their image of themselves and become high in their own eyes. They have less far to fall in order to take their place at the feet of the Saviour.

At the same time they are **less pre-occupied with the affairs of this life**. They are not burdened with the responsibilities of business and domestic work, nor have they discovered the vast variety of pleasure pursuits to distract them and absorb their time and energy. They are also far from that time of life when human powers begin to fail and a negative attitude to life develops. It was this thought that prompted the Preacher (Ecclesiastes) to counsel the young to turn to God in their early days, before the natural powers decay.[32]

In addition to this, children are by nature **more responsive** to teaching and invitation. They can equally respond to false teaching and invitations to sin, which makes it the more urgent that their natural responsiveness is directed to the right ends. Inasmuch as the gospel is about receiving knowledge and acting upon it, these come quite naturally to them. Just as education is given during the first dozen or so years because they will receive, retain and respond to it, so it is with the gospel. Whether or not it saves them, they will be able to learn it and become interested in it. The minds of children are free from the accumulated clutter which years of acquired knowledge, ideas, opinions and theories build up in the minds of adults. They

will not see all the problems and objections that cloud the minds of
their elders. Truths sown in them will go deep and remain, like seed
in the soft crumbly soil. They don't need double digging, and once
implanted the truth is not quickly driven out by a host of other
thoughts crowding in.

Children are also generally **submissive**. They quickly realise
they are under authority and that the best way to get by is by doing
what their parents tell them. They have not reached the stage when
independence and autonomy are the thing. At this stage the idea of
God as a heavenly parent does not seem strange or objectionable.
Indeed it is far more natural than for the adult who has long forgotten
the days when he had to trust that Dad and Mum know best.

They also tend to be **trusting**. They have not developed the
cynicism that comes from being frequently let down. They take
offers and promises at their face value. They have not become
complicated by the suspiciousness with which the adult views
'Greeks bearing gifts'. They take us at our word and hold us to our
promises. If we don't keep them they undergo the nearest thing a
child can have to a nervous breakdown. So if they are told God
promises them a place in his kingdom as his children if they come
to Jesus, they are not going to doubt whether he means it.

Most relevant of all, perhaps, they are **helpless**, and the younger
they are the truer this is. They do not have the pride which stands in
the way of letting someone do something for them or of receiving
a gift without strings or cost. Is this not the spirit in which we are all
to receive the kingdom? Is this not what Jesus meant when he said,
'Anyone who will not receive the kingdom of God as a little child
will never enter it' (Mark 10:15)? He meant we have to stop relying
on our natural goodness, our righteousness, our good works, our
knowledge and so forth, and come to him with 'nothing in our
hands'. Who is more disposed to this than a little child?

We can therefore say with S. D. Burchard: 'Childhood is therefore peculiarly and emphatically the age designed by God in the
constitution of things, designated by the Scriptures and demonstrated by experience as the time for the successful application of the
means of grace; the spring time, the time for sowing the good seed
of the word, the time which above all others invites effort and gives
promise of success'.[33]

Far from not having the capacity to respond to the call of the
gospel, therefore, children probably have a greater capacity than

adults. This does not mean they require any less enabling from the Holy Spirit than anyone else. Regeneration is a work of God which he performs in whomsoever he will by the operation of his power. From **his** standpoint it is no 'harder' to save a ninety-year-old than it is a nine-year-old. Nevertheless from **our** standpoint times and conditions have a part to play. Didn't Jesus say it is hard for a rich man to enter the kingdom? By this he did not mean God found it hard, for he immediately went on to say, 'What is impossible with men is possible with God'.[34] He meant that for such to respond involved a great deal of pain and sacrifice. He would have to change both his lifestyle and his whole way of thinking. His riches would be a hindrance to this.

Young children do not have such hindrances. They still need divine grace to enable them to learn and grasp the truth of the gospel, but there will be less for them to unlearn. They have less to give up, very little that can be called sacrifice to make. To them conversion won't be such a struggle. It is right for us to make good use of this condition of life while it lasts and to do all we can to teach them and encourage them to respond. This state of things will not last long. But we need to know how to take advantage of it, and to this we will now proceed.

C. THE MEANS OF A CHILD'S CONVERSION

Believing parents are in a unique position to take full advantage of the capacity of a child to respond to the gospel. We have them with us from their conception right through to early adulthood. We need be in no hurry and can use the full range of means at our disposal.

1. Prayer

Hannah, Samuel's mother, first prayed that she would have a child. This is indicated in the meaning of his name, 'She called him Samuel, saying, "Because I asked the Lord for him"' (1 Sam. 1:20). Since she had long been infertile she regarded her conception, if not as miraculous, yet as a special act of God. This she acknowledged in the promise which accompanied her prayer — that she would 'give him to the Lord all the days of his life' (1 Sam. 1:11). Setting aside the unique aspects of the story, we learn basically to ask God to bless our marriages and homes with children, whom we regard always as his gift.[35] Although we don't make bargains with God (and Hannah was not doing this) we offer back to him any children he is pleased to give us, so that they might belong to him even more than they do to us.

On their birth we make a specific dedication of them to him, which may or may not include a public one in the church. Paedo-baptists have them baptised, believing as they do that they are already in covenant relationship with God. Baptists do not share this conviction, but are no less hopeful that God will hear their prayer and make their children his. Some express this hope in a dedication service in church, in which they not only commit the child to God but themselves as parents.[36] All through the years of 'irresponsibil-ity' they continue to pray for them. They do so with the assurance that God makes special provision for children during these years and that his angelic guard is as much over them as it is over those of maturer years. They are also praying that God will prepare them to instruct the child as he becomes capable of receiving it, and will prepare the child for this instruction. Although we do not know how it works, there can be no question that this prayer backing has a real effect on the child as well as on how the parents handle him.

2. Teaching

As with other childhood matters, teaching the truth of the gospel will be done gradually. Although Isaiah was being ironic in 28:9f in order to rebuke the Israelites for learning at the rate of children when they should be taking it in like adults, his words do give some insight into how to teach young children: 'here a little, there a little'. The rate can be as slow as necessary. The important thing is that what is taught is the gospel and not some mythical form of religion akin to fairies and Father Christmas.

There is no need to withhold the basic facts because they are young. At the same time these should not be over-elaborated. Bob Sheehan has written: 'There is sometimes confusion in our thinking between the amount a person knows when he is saved (which varies vastly) and the amount a person needs to know to be saved ... Whether as a child or an adult, a person needs to understand his sinfulness, who the Saviour is and to call on him for salvation. Nothing more is necessary'.[37]

A century ago Henry C. Fish in his *Handbook of Revivals* expressed substantially the same view: 'The gospel is comprehended in these two facts: man a sinner and Christ a Saviour ... And cannot a child comprehend these two simple facts? When an infant it understands what it is to disobey and displease a parent and feel sorry for it. Is it difficult to impart the idea that God may be disobeyed and what it is to be penitent in view of it? A very young child may understand this. And why not also that Christ is a Saviour?'.[38]

More specifically, there are three areas on which to concentrate:

a. Sin

We have already established the fact that children are sinners, even before they 'transgress', by virtue of their descent from Adam. They can be taught the story of creation and the Fall in this way and be shown how it makes them sinners. There is no need to accuse them of more adult sins in order to produce adult conviction. At the same time they can be warned that because of the Fall they are weak and likely to commit these more serious sins before long. We can explain that their occasional (or frequent!) naughtiness and disobedience, their childish sins, are all the result of Adam's fall and if something isn't done, this state of affairs will get worse.

b. Judgement

There is no need to lay this on with a trowel and paint a lurid picture of hell in order to frighten them into repentance. At best this will produce self-righteous goodness, at worst put them off the Bible for life. Use the analogy between yourself and your heavenly parent. You are displeased when your children are naughty and you show it. The child feels this as well as you and it affects your relationship with each other. The same happened with Adam. The story shows how grieved God was when Adam and Eve disobeyed him, how they felt this and hid from him, as a child may do when he has been naughty. God had to question Adam to get him to own up, and then to punish him. There is nothing very difficult in getting a child to identify with this scenario! Other Bible stories, such as the Flood and the lives of the great characters of Old and New Testaments, can be used to back this up. They all sinned against God, displeased him and suffered the consequences. Most of all, they lost his favour.

c. Salvation

Again we can begin in Eden. There God offered Adam and Eve a way out of their mess. Not one that **they** could find; it had to be brought to them. God promised that one would come who would break the hold that sin had gained over them and even take the punishment for it. This One came. His name is Jesus. He came to find those who had lost their way to God. Children understand and love 'lost and found' stories and none is better than those Jesus told in Luke 15. But he had to go on to suffer and die to find and save us. Now he is alive again. He is here. He is near.

These, then, are the facts. Now what about the response?

3. Encouragement

The question of the response of young children to the gospel is the trickiest aspect of the whole matter and it is not surprising to find differences of view. Inviting them to 'make a decision' is not so universally advocated by evangelicals as in the past.

Those who hold the view that all children belong to God approach the matter in a different way from those who believe they are away from God, lost in sin. Ron Buckland puts the former view forward in these words: 'By maintaining all children begin with God ... the style and stance of evangelism changes. This is captured by John Inchley who argues that the question to ask children is not "Have you said 'Yes' to Jesus?" but "Have you said 'No' to Jesus"'.[39] Buckland therefore comes out against decisions for Christ and prefers to talk of 'decisions **towards** Christ'. 'It is my belief', he writes, 'that many people, including children, make decisions **towards** Christ, rather than making a once-for-all decision to follow Christ. I see these gradual steps into dawning light becoming that radical reorientation of life called Christian discipleship'.[40] 'Most people grow into faith ... We must not think only in terms of one moment of response. The Christian life is an ongoing series of responses to God'.[41]

This does not mean these writers believe that a response in children in unnecessary. Rather that there is a danger of stereotyping it. Inchley surveys the ways in which Jesus in the Gospels called for response.[42] Matthew was called to 'follow' him, while Zaccheus 'welcomed him'. Elsewhere he spoke of 'entering' as through a door, or 'receiving' him by 'believing his name'. Inchley likens saying 'I will' to Christ's invitation to what a man and woman do in marrying. One form to be avoided is 'giving your heart to Jesus', partly because Jesus never used it and partly because of the literalistic attitude of children towards their bodily organs.[43]

The problem here is that in almost every case the invitations of Jesus are addressed to adults, people familiar with Bible language or at least with figurative speech. This is why it is probably best to concentrate on the one occasion when he did adapt his call to children. When 'little children were brought to Jesus' and the disciples tried to intervene, he said, 'Let the little children **come** to me' (Matt. 19:13f). He used the same metaphor when speaking to those who were 'little children' in a spiritual sense, that is, those to whom God had revealed his word because they were prepared to adopt a childlike attitude towards him: 'Come to me, all you who are weary and burdened, and I will give you rest' (Matt. 11:25-30). He also used the illustrations of sheep coming to their shepherd at the sound of his voice[44] and chicks coming under the mother hen's wings when something frightened them.[45]

Language of this kind has the advantage of being well within the range of a child's comprehension. To 'come' means more to a child than to 'believe'. Believing is an abstract idea that takes place in the mind. Coming is an action which they themselves continually perform. From early days they have 'come' to their parents and fallen into their arms. This is how they begin to learn movement and eventually to walk and run. 'Coming' combines the elements of need, trust and love, and these comprise faith. 'Coming' is motivated by the prospect of safety, comfort, provision and protection which will be found in the one to whom he 'comes'. Thus children can be taught 'faith' even without using that (to them) difficult word.

We can encourage our children to think of Jesus as waiting to welcome them in order to save them from that sinful state inherited from Adam, and to bring them back into God's favour; to think of him as he was that day when the young were brought to him and he took them in his arms. Without necessarily using words like 'repent' and 'believe', this is what we have been talking about. Moreover, we have turned their thoughts from ourselves to him. We are not trying to get them to obey or please us, but to respond to him.

We must be sure that we don't pressurise but gently encourage them. Says Bob Sheehan, 'The natural responsiveness of children requires great care on our part. Many have memories of being "evangelised" as children. Children's responses to the plea to "believe in Jesus" can be motivated by all sorts of childish reasons. Some are very keen to please. Others are too timid to disobey'.[37] Ron Buckland says he 'counselled a twenty-two-year-old man who said he had made "decisions for Christ" at the ages of nine, fourteen and eighteen'. In his own understanding he had been converted three times and it hadn't worked.[46]

   We can obviate this problem by the gentle and gradual approach. We need not tell them to 'come **now**' unless they specifically ask. 'Coming' doesn't have to be a sudden, decisive, one-off act. We do not need to interrogate them with questions like, 'Have you done it yet?' Coming to Jesus is not an 'it' like washing your face or making your bed. It is a developing attitude. It continues. We keep coming. The first occasion may get lost in the mists of time. If we have been praying for our children since conception, praying over and with them since birth, telling them the simple facts from the dawn of verbal communication, and gently encouraging them to look on Jesus as the one who died to bring them to God and waits for them to trust themselves to him, as lambs and chicks do to their mothers, then what we call 'conversion' may take place without our conscious awareness, and even without their realising its full significance at the time.

   This is not important and it won't bother us provided we, like the parents in Matthew 19, have in prayer 'brought them to Jesus'. We shall be trusting that in his own way and time he will take them to himself. Gradually it will appear that they are his. They will be heard expressing their thanks to Jesus for dying for them. There are few better signs of life than this — far better than bragging about a 'decision'. They will also become more interested in finding ways of pleasing him. They can then be taught that while they are very young what pleases him most is loving obedience to you as parents. This was how Paul counselled the children in the churches to which he wrote.[47] The children to whom he addressed these words were 'in the Lord' — they had heard his call and come to him; they were thankful for his saving death. This is the way for them to show that thankfulness — by obeying their parents. Paul clearly believed in child conversion through the patient praying and teaching of the parents. It is good to know that encouraging our children to come to Christ is part of the apostolic faith.

References

Section II; Part II, A
1 *Guidelines for Christian Parents*
2 *Realities of Childhood*, pp. 108-109
3 'Crises of the Christ', quoted in the above, p. 109
4 Inchley, op. cit. p. 21
5 *Children and the King*, p. 70
6 John 2:23-25
7 See also 1 Cor. 5:5; 7:28; 2 Cor. 10:11; Gal. 6:1; Titus 3:11
8 *Children and God*, pp. 16-17
9 Pridmore, op. cit. p. 130
10 See Gal. 4:1-2
11 *Systematic Theology*, pp. 287-288
12 *Christian Baptism*, p. 68
13 *Institutes*, IV. xvi. 15.
14 Acts 1:4; John 14:16f; Luke 24:49
15 R. B. Rackham, *Acts of the Apostles* in loc.
16 D. Kingdon: *Children of Abraham*, p. 93
17 *Ibid.* p. 94

Section II; Part II, B
18 Mark 10:13
19 *Children and the King*, p. 8
20 Jer. 1:5
21 Gen. 18:10; Jud. 13:5; 2 Kings 4:16; Luke 1:13
22 1 Sam. 1:20
23 1 Sam. 2
24 1 Sam. 3:2-10
25 1 Sam. 3:11-14
26 1 Sam. 3:19-21
27 Matt. 21:16
28 Acts 2:17f
29 Quoted in *Sword and Trowel*, 1992, No:2
30 *To be near unto God*, p. 655
31 Matt. 18:1-4
32 Ecc. 12:1-8
33 Quoted in Henry C. Fish:*Handbook of Revivals*, p. 172
34 Luke 18:24-27

Section II; Part II, C
35 Ps. 127:3
36 Public dedication will be looked at more fully in pp. 139-140
37 'Original Sin and Children' in *Reformation Today* No: 128
38 Gano Books, 1988, pp. 168-169
39 *Children and God*, p. 48
40 *Ibid.* p. 51
41 *Ibid.* pp. 52-53
42 *Realities of Childhood*, p. 114
43 *Ibid.* p. 119
44 John 10:27
45 Luke 13:34
46 op. cit. p. 52
47 Eph. 6:1-3; Col. 3:20

Section III:
Children and the home

On the subject of our children's relationship with us as parents the Bible seems to have all too little to say. The consequence of this is that we find many of our questions on the matter hard to answer. A further result is the sharp disagreement there is over the answers to these questions.

One thing is clear and we shall all agree with it. From the time our children make their very obvious entrance into our homes, our happiness is inextricably bound up with how they turn out: their character, behaviour, approach to life and their enjoyment of it or otherwise. The Book of Proverbs, that manual of parental instruction, gives us some very powerful warnings on this point — indeed, this is how the proverbs proper begin: 'A wise son brings joy to his father, but a foolish son grief to his mother' (10:1).[1]

With all this in mind we shall look at three big questions:

1. What is a Christian family?
2. Are the children of Christians different from others?
3. What are our responsibilities to our children?

A. THE CHRISTIAN FAMILY

When Christians marry and start having children, the phrase 'Christian family' begins to be used of them. But what is it? Is there such a thing? How do we define it? What constitutes it? Must both parents be Christians? Is one sufficient? Is it only 'Christian' when the children come to personal faith? If so, must all of them believe before the phrase can be applied to them, or is it enough if one or more believes?

In the absence of a biblical definition, which seems to be wanting, let us proceed by logic. The average family is usually defined as two adults of opposite sexes plus 2.4 children. A 'Christian family' then would be two believing adults plus two or three believing children. But of how many homes is this true? Many children of believing parents do not come to faith until their teens or later. Some parents will say quite openly that they are still praying for the conversion of their children. Does this mean that for the first dozen or so years of their children's lives it was not a 'Christian family'? What about a family in which all the children have come to faith and then another is born? Do they revert from being a Christian to a non-Christian family?

How can we answer these questions? It will help if we look successively at the Old and New Testaments.

1. The Old Testament

The term 'family' occurs frequently in the Old Testament and is easily defined. Two members of the nation came together in marriage — usually from the same 'line', that is, both had the same son of Jacob for their ancestor. Any children born to them were Israelites, not merely in the ethnic and national sense, but religiously too. Israel was in covenant with God and the children were included. This was why all males were circumcised on the eighth day of their lives. It was in this way God continued to have a people of his own down the centuries, and how their number increased — 'in the line of continued generations'. 'From everlasting to everlasting the Lord's love is with those who fear him, and his righteousness with their children's children, with those who keep his covenant and remember to obey his precepts' (Ps. 103:17-18). As Malachi put it when chiding the people after their return from Babylon for divorcing their partners: 'You have broken faith with her (your wife) though she is your partner, the wife of your marriage covenant. Has not the Lord made them one? In flesh and spirit they are his. And why one? Because he was seeking a godly offspring' — literally 'an offspring of God' (Mal. 2:14f).

Abraham, the founder of the nation, had realised this centuries before Israel came into existence when he complained to God that his promise to form 'a great nation' of which he would be father ('Abram' means 'great father') could not be fulfilled while he lacked a male heir.[2] The rest of Genesis is in the same vein. The thread running through it is marriage within the clan, the circumcision of the resulting children, then their marriages. This process is repeated through the lines of Isaac, Jacob and his twelve sons, especially Joseph.

Abraham and Isaac both went to great lengths to ensure right marriages for their sons. The failure of Esau to marry within the godly clan was a source of grief to Isaac and Rebekah.[3] Much of the story of Jacob revolves around his various 'marriages' and the resulting children. On one occasion it appeared advantageous that his children should intermarry with the Shechemites in the interests of peace and prosperity. Although Jacob consented it never came about — in fact it was prevented in a most barbarous fashion.[4] Although the behaviour of Simeon and Levi was reprehensible, there is something of divine providence and even judgement in the drastic way the plan miscarried. It was not God's will for Abraham's descendants to become mixed with another people.

We don't know much about the wives of Jacob's sons since the interest of the story after Shechem centres around Joseph. But in Genesis 46, when Jacob's life up to his departure for Egypt is being summed up, we read of his grandsons and grand-daughters who went with him. This indicates that the underlying theme of Genesis since Abraham has been the maintaining of the covenant nation through the bloodline of Abraham.

Later generations learned to see this as the way the Lord 'built his house' (Ps. 127:1) — his family or nation. The sons born to the families of such a nation were the special gift of God, 'a heritage from the Lord ... a reward from him' (Ps. 127:3). They were 'like arrows in the hands of a warrior' because they made them feel unashamed 'when they contend with their enemies in the gate' (Ps. 127:5). This was because they knew that, having sons given by God to his people, they could be sure the nation would continue and its enemies be defeated.

With the children of Israelite parents there was no question in their minds about 'would they come to believe or not?' Their membership of the nation was not based on personal faith but birth and circumcision. As they grew up they were taught about belief and obedience, but whatever they thought or did they remained Israelites. So the families were united. The task of the parents was to teach them the nation's history and laws.[5] They needed to know what it meant to be of an Israelite family. They were so bound together that, while in their children's early days the parents could be held responsible for their children's behaviour, later the situation might be reversed.[6]

So all the children of the nation were Israelite by birth and circumcision. There was family unity. You could speak of 'an Israelite family' or even 'a godly family'.

2. The New Testament

There are those who believe you can talk of 'the Christian family' in the same way as you can of the Israelite family, because they believe God continues to work 'along the lines of continued generations'. Herman Hanko, for example, finds evidence for this in two places: (a) In 'specific commands of God to children to come as well as adults'. If Jesus invited children (even babies) to come to him as well as their parents, this indicates the situation is unchanged. He would only ask them to come if they were already his. (b) In the application of the fifth commandment to children by Paul in Ephesians 6:1-3. Originally, he says, the fifth commandment was addressed to those who 'have the Lord for their God' (Exod. 20:12) 'which therefore includes children to whom the commandment is addressed'.[7] This would seem to mean that if the fifth commandment is preached to children, as it was by Paul in Ephesians 6, or by parents at home, it proves they belong to God, just as they did under the old covenant. This makes the Christian family the counterpart of the Israelite family.

There are some problems with this argument.

a. *It implies that the commandment cannot be taught to the children of non-Christians,* who do not 'have the Lord for their God' (Exod. 20:12). Does this mean that such are under no obligation to obey their parents? Surely the commandment given to Israel represents a perpetual and universal moral absolute for which all must give account, since it appears all will be judged by it.[8] Why then is it addressed to those who 'have the Lord for their God'? The answer is that the Ten Commandments represent God's covenant agreement with Israel. They are not themselves the universal moral absolutes, but an adaptation of them for the covenant people for the period of time in which they held that status. But for children to obey their parents is part of that universal natural law written on all consciences.[9] Even the most ignorant non-Christian parents require obedience and their children practise it. So this is no argument for drawing a parallel between the Israelite and Christian family.

b. *Christian culture has altered the whole concept of what constitutes a family.* We think in terms of 'the nuclear family', but the Israelite conception was far broader. The whole nation which descended from its original ancestor was 'one family' (Amos 3:1). While from the practical standpoint those who lived under one roof were 'a family', from the religious angle they derived their identity from membership of the national family (Amos 3:2). 'The family in the Old Testament could refer to the father's house, the extended family or even the nation as a whole.[10] There is no biblical word for the nuclear family, although the fifth commandment shows it was recognised as a central part of the household'.[11] This concept became general in oriental society and persists today. Several generations live under one roof or close together and constitute 'a family' or 'household'. At one time even slaves were part of it.

c. *The new covenant operates differently from the old.* God works not through physical but through spiritual birth. This manifests itself not in circumcision but conversion. In Colossians 2:12 Paul describes New Testament circumcision as 'putting off the sinful nature' (through repentance), followed by union with Christ in his death and burial (through faith). This is performed not 'by the hands of men but with the circumcision done by Christ', an essentially spiritual and divine action. Baptism is mentioned because it is a dramatic expression of repentance and faith-union with Christ, but it is not the means of it.

This 'circumcision' is not automatically performed on the children of Christians, and is also open to other children and adults, which may be why the New Testament does not speak of 'the Christian family', for you never know where God is going to work and whom he is going to call. He may pass our children by and call someone down the road who never heard of Christ from his parents. It is also the reason why we have different aims for our children from those of the Israelites. We want not only to teach them the laws and history of the people of God in Old and New Testaments but to see them come to personal faith, followed by spiritual growth. The Old Testament will give us some help here but it will be limited.

In this connection it is interesting to observe that when Paul preached the fifth commandment to children in the congregations to which he wrote, he changed its wording. In Ephesians 6:1-3, instead of saying 'that your life may be long in the land the Lord your God is giving you' (Exod. 20:12), he says 'that you may enjoy long life on earth'. He not only omits the reference to 'the Lord your God' which Hanko finds so significant, but alters 'land' to 'earth'. Paul in the gospel age no longer thought in terms of that special land which was at the heart of the old covenant.[12] He thought of people all over 'the earth' becoming God's covenant people. Moreover he actually paraphrases the original commandment in v. 1 in the words 'Children obey your parents in the Lord'. The phrase 'in the Lord' normally means 'in a personal relationship with the Lord Jesus Christ'. He is speaking to children who have what we call 'Christian parents'. The obligation to obedience is a moral absolute which applies under the gospel, although it is differently expressed.

Moreover the motivation is different. In Ephesians 6 Paul's paraphrase of it is 'this is right', and in Colossians 3 'this pleases the Lord' (Christ). These alterations show that obedience to parents is important under the new covenant for different reasons from what it was under the old covenant. Then it was vital for the continuance of the nation 'in the land the Lord your God is giving you'. It was essential to the continuance of the godly line. Now that the question of who occupies ancient Canaan is irrelevant to the gospel, this is no longer the reason for the obligation to obedience. The reason now is a spiritual one — personal relationship with the Lord Jesus Christ. The phrases 'in the Lord', 'right' (in the Lord's eyes) and 'this pleases the Lord' are not about land tenure but about relationship with God. This reflects the great change in the covenants. The old was about a special nation possessing a special land, the new is about personal relationship with God through Christ for people of all lands or none at all.

All this must be taken into account when we use a phrase like 'the Christian family'. It is a far less precise unit than 'the Israelite family'. It is rather like 'a Christian country'. This cannot mean a country where all are Christians, for it is unlikely that this ever happens. A state cannot decide the religious allegiance of each of its citizens. There are those who try to do this and claim to have succeeded. In today's world these are mainly Islamic countries like Iran and Saudi Arabia, which we therefore call 'theocracies'. But it is doubtful whether all the citizens of these nations truly believe and practise Islam, although those who don't probably keep quiet about it. It has happened in Christianity that a state has committed itself to this faith and enforced church attendance. This has been tried in Britain but soon found to be unworkable. The most we can mean by 'a Christian country' is that it is one in which Christianity is the majority religion and whose institutions are strongly influenced by Christian standards and values.

Used in this sense there may be some value in speaking of 'a Christian family'. It indicates that at least one parent is a Christian and is attempting to teach the rest of the family to adopt Christian principles and practices: to worship God through Christ, to know and believe the Bible and to follow the ethics of the New Testament. It should not be taken to imply that because one or both parents are committed to Christ, the whole family is truly Christian. But it does show that that parent or those parents recognise they cannot just live to themselves as Christians, but have responsibilities to their children and/or spouse. It means that their offspring come into a different category from that of the non-Christians' children, a subject to which we now turn.

B. SPECIAL CHILDREN

The question here is whether the children of Christian parents are different from others and if so in what sense or senses.

1. How they are the same

To be consistent with the principles already stated about the nature of children as taught in the Bible, we must say there are certain ways in which our children are the same as those of others.

a. *Like others they come into the world spiritually dead and therefore away from God.* This applies right across the board. As in Old Testament times it was true of Israelite as well as Gentile children, so now it is true of those of Christian parents as well as those of non-Christians. This means all alike need regeneration.

There is a considerable degree of agreement on this among Evangelicals. John Inchley holds clearly and strongly that all children are 'in the kingdom of God' and 'included in the great atoning sacrifice', a view that has been disputed in these pages.

However, when he writes 'that godly believing parents should prayerfully expect this sovereign work of regeneration will be happening in the lives of their children at a very early age'[13] he must believe they begin spiritually dead, however short the period in which they remain in that state, otherwise it would not be necessary to use the term 'regeneration' of them at all. How this accords with their being 'in the kingdom' is his problem, but such as he are clearly reluctant to abandon altogether the doctrine of 'original sin' and human depravity. Christ's 'no one can see the kingdom of God unless he is born again' (John 3:3) has a powerful hold on the minds of Bible-believing teachers, however much they try to qualify it.

b. *They cannot be saved or regenerated through the faith of their parents.* Faith cannot be transmitted from parent to child in such a way as to bring them to regeneration. According to Jesus only God can do this work. Those who become 'children of God ... are born not of natural descent, nor of human decision or a husband's will, but born of God' (John 1:12f). God's hand cannot be directed in this. It is like the wind which 'blows wherever it pleases. You hear its sound, but you cannot tell where it comes from or where it is going' (John 3:8). We Christian parents are as impotent as non-Christian parents in this matter.

There are signs that John Inchley, with his great regard for Horace Bushnell, is inclined to think that parental activity does have that effect. He quotes Bushnell with approval, 'It is the privilege and duty of every Christian parent that his children shall come forth into action as a regenerate stock. The organic unity is to be a power of life'.[14] It is this that leads him to say the words quoted above about expecting the work of regeneration to be taking place at an early age. He seems to see regeneration happening by some mysterious transmission of the life of the parent to the child. Later he refers to instances in the New Testament in which 'the household and family is included in the blessing of salvation which has been experienced by a father or mother: Zacchaeus (Luke 19), the nobleman (John 4), Onesiphorus (2 Tim. 1:16) and the Philippian gaoler (Acts 16). In the case of Timothy he sees the transmission as occurring over three generations — from grandmother to mother to son (2 Tim. 1:5)'.[15]

Yet he goes on to speak of it as 'the unconditional and sovereign work of God' and quotes John 3:8. Then he quotes Bishop Ryle's 'The change is one which no man can give to himself nor yet to another. It would be as reasonable to expect the dead to raise themselves or to require an artist to give a statue life'.[16] The Bishop and Bushnell do not seem to be saying the same thing and it requires a theological contortionist to make them agree. Such are the ambiguities into which thinkers can get themselves on this matter.

c. *Baptism at any age cannot regenerate them.* The 'washing of rebirth' written of by Paul in Titus 3:5 is not baptism. It refers to the cleansing effect of the work of regeneration on the sinful nature. The Spirit makes us clean, as Ezekiel predicted.[17] It could have been these words Jesus had in mind when he spoke to Nicodemus about being 'born of water and the Spirit' (John 3:5). He was not necessarily referring to two actions — baptism in water and baptism in the Spirit. To separate two things which belong together was the poetic Hebrew way of speaking. To be born of the Spirit includes being washed clean of the pollution of sin. It is true that baptism symbolises the washing away of sin, but this is simply 'the outward and visible sign of an inward and spiritual grace', the sign that repentance and faith have taken place. When Paul came to repentance and faith he was encouraged to 'Get up, be baptised and wash away your sin, calling on his name' (Acts 22:16). The work of regeneration, producing repentance and faith, had already washed his sins away and he could now confess it and receive assurance through baptism.

Spurgeon in his famous sermon of 1864 warns parents about trusting in baptism and neglecting to teach their children the necessity of the new birth. He draws attention to a contemporary hymn which was giving false comfort to some:

> 'Though thy conception was in sin,
> A sacred bathing thou hast had;
> And though thy birth unclean has been,
> A blameless babe thou now are made.
> Sweet baby, then forbear to weep;
> Be still, my dear sweet baby, sleep'. [18]

Much as it would be lovely to believe the contrary, our children are the same after baptism as before.

d. *We cannot treat them as 'little Christians'* who have the spiritual abilities of other Christians only on a smaller scale. We cannot expect them to understand the doctrines of Scripture, although they can enjoy its stories as we read or tell them. We cannot expect them to pray in the Spirit, even though we may get them to repeat prayers such as the Lord's Prayer, or even compose their own. We cannot expect them to respond to the spiritual commands of Christ, and we need to be careful we don't overdo calling on them to 'come to him', of which an earlier chapter spoke. As pointed out, there is a danger of their saying they have 'come' because we have asked them to. They may equate it with our other calls on them and regard it as part of the obedience due to parents.

On the other hand, if they are in that disobedient and rebellious frame of mind we've all been through, that refuses to do something for no better reason than that a parent asks it, they may apply this to their response to the gospel call when they don't really mean to. The result will be confusing to them and us. We must accept that our doctrine of 'spiritual inability' applies to our children as it did to us before we began to experience the workings of the Spirit in regeneration.

In these respects, then, our children are in the same boat as those of others. But this does not mean they are in no way different, and it is this difference we must now explore.

2. How they are different

A good way to see this is to go back to a passage already discussed: 1 Corinthians 7:14. On that occasion we had to show what it did **not** mean.[19] Some interpret it as meaning that children are included in the covenant through their parents' faith. Because of this their fallen and sinful nature does not prevent their having a relationship with God. This interpretation needed refuting. Now we can be more positive and show that it does make our children 'special', even if it doesn't teach their inclusion in the covenant.

a. They are special as God's gifts to his children

They are 'holy' (Greek: *hagios*) in the same way as every gift from God is 'holy' to those who acknowledge his generosity and thank him. In 1 Timothy 4:3-4 Paul denounces those (presumably professing Christians) who would come to despise marriage and certain foods, regarding them as 'unholy'. Paul's reply is that believers who know the truth are of all people most qualified to enjoy these as he intended — that is, to receive them 'with thanksgiving'. They do this: i) by **believing** what 'the word of God' says about God's works in creation, how they came from him in a perfect condition and for our enjoyment and our need; and ii) by **doing** what the word of God says we should do, which is to use them according to his rules, especially by praying about them — asking him for our daily bread and thanking him for it.

Those who do this 'sanctify' them, they make them 'holy' (Greek: *hagiazetai*). This cannot mean they are brought into covenant relationship with God or are morally purified, both of which ideas are inappropriate to such things. It can only mean that in the case of the thankful believer these gifts of God are used as he originally intended — as coming from his hands for our good. He may give them to the unbeliever just as freely, but the unbeliever does not acknowledge or thank him, and may even abuse them by greed, lust or waste.

The 'holiness' of believers' children is parallel to this. Like the Israelites they see them as God's gift [20] and thank him for them. They understand and accept what God's word says about them and seek to obey it in the way they treat them. They make them a matter of 'prayer', from the time they were just a twinkle in their eyes, right through their birth and upbringing on into adulthood. Unbelievers don't do this. To them children are not God's gifts. To some, alas, they are an unwanted nuisance, to be disposed of by abortion, or, if they accept them, to be kept as much as possible out of the way, or even abused. To others, who passionately want children, they are human rights and must be obtained at all costs. Instead of praying for them and accepting God's 'Yes' or 'No', they use every facility known to modern science to induce fertility.

Not that fertility treatment is in itself wrong for a Christian. As with most 'neutral' things all depends on attitude. A believing couple may certainly pursue all avenues that are not contradictory to biblical principles in order to bear children, but they will still recognise that the ultimate ability to procreate is from God, and will not feel cheated if this is withheld. If normal or abnormal methods are successful they will give him the credit and thank him. Possibly, if the road has been long and hard and they have had to spend time

and money on fertility treatment, they will feel even more thankful
than a couple who have had no trouble, and have even had to use
means to prevent or space out births.

   Just as before and at the birth they sought to proceed according
to 'God's word', so after the birth they continue to do so in their
treatment and upbringing, about which more will be said later. But
these are the ways in which the children of believing parents are
'holy' — in the way they are seen as coming from God and are
treated as his gifts. This is something 'special' to believers, about
which unbelievers know little.

b. They are special as 'set apart' for God's blessing

'Set apart' is often the meaning of 'sanctified'. Under the old
covenant mountains, cities, buildings, utensils and so on were
'consecrated to God' for his use; but under the new covenant it is
people rather than places and things that are set apart. It is in this
sense as well as the other that believers' children are 'holy' — they
are consecrated or given back to God, as Hannah gave Samuel to
God, so that he will take them for his own and bless them if he will.
Whatever he does or does not do with them, they certainly find
themselves in the places where God's blessing comes, for they have
access to the means he normally uses to bestow blessing. Far from
the children of Christians being less privileged than Israelite ones
because they don't baptise them where the Israelites circumcised
them, they are in fact more privileged. 'The children born into
Christian households enjoy from the beginning the better promises
mediated direct from Christ and held forth in the administration of
the gospel, a situation immeasurably superior to that of the children
of Leah'.[21]

   Here are some of the privileges which make believers' children
'special' and give them access to the means of God's blessing.

1. They hear the word of God. This will happen chiefly at home,
in their family or bedside prayers when the stories or teachings are
simply and directly addressed to them. They will also hear it
indirectly as their parents converse with each other or their friends.
In this way at least they resemble Israelite children.[22] However, the
things they hear from their parents were unknown to Israelite
children, especially the birth, life, death and resurrection of the

promised Messiah. They will also hear more of the same at their parents' church as they grow older.

2. *They are prayed for and with*. They will hear their names linked with God's and Christ's as his protection is asked for them and his blessing sought upon them. When out of sight and hearing — awake or asleep — they will still be upheld in their parents' prayers.

'I hope many of us, as soon as our children saw the light, if not before, presented them to God with this anxious prayer, that they might sooner die than live to disgrace their father's God. We only desired children that we might in them live over again another life of service to God; and when we looked into their young faces, we never asked wealth for them, nor fame nor anything else but that they might be dear unto God, and that their names might be written in the Lamb's Book of Life. We did then bring our children to Christ as far as we could do it by presenting them before God by earnest prayer on their behalf'.[23]

3. *They are exposed to the example of one or both parents*. Proverbs 20:7 speaks of the power of parental example thus: 'The righteous man leads a blameless life: blessed are his children after him.' While this will teach them many things, the chief one will be the love of God. Their parents' loving care of them will teach them of God's loving care. Until he is a personal reality to them they will experience his love in that of their parents. Also their parents' loving care of each other will teach them about Christ's love for his church, of which marital love is a symbol. They will see that love expressed outside the family as they witness the love of members of the local church for each other. Since love is the fruit of faith, these examples will encourage them to believe for themselves, for it will make faith more attractive to them.

4. *They will feel a sense of God's presence in their home*. Where there is love between parents and between them and their children, and where God is prayed to and spoken of, an atmosphere is created. The growing child will gradually sense the difference between this and what he finds in other homes or places where people gather. It will be a powerful incentive to him to come and seek God for himself. 'We must reject the idea that the sole criterion for the existence of a Christian family is that one or both parents profess faith in Christ. A Christian family is not simply measured by externals, but is marked by a warm cohesiveness in which **relation-ships** and **atmosphere** are Christian'.[24] 'There is an awareness of Christ in a home where everything is God-centred'.[25]

Thus the home becomes a greenhouse in which spiritual life can be born and begin to grow. 'What advantage then do our children have over those who are born to unbelieving homes? ... Salvation is near to our children. It is right by them. In the case of those born into non-Christian homes, the prospect is terrifying because everything militates against their coming to understand, trust in Christ and believe in the Scriptures. Ignorance prevails ... Christian parents can be encouraged to think upon the fact that the Lord who plans from eternity and orders all things well, has already caused our children to be born into the circle where grace is mediated'.[26]

C. OUR RESPONSIBILITIES TO OUR CHILDREN

We have just seen that some Christians, while they do not see their children as covenant children, still regard them as special. Special children require special treatment. Special treatment involves special responsibilities. The relevant Scripture passages indicate three main areas in which those responsibilities lie.

1. We are to care for them as God cares for us

There is a passage in the Sermon on the Mount in which Jesus is encouraging his disciples to pray with expectancy: 'Ask and it will be given to you; seek and you will find; knock and the door will be opened to you ...' (Matt. 7:7-11). To make this more vibrant he draws an analogy between God's treatment of us and ours of our children. When they are hungry and ask for food we give them something edible and nourishing. Although the main thrust of his words concerns the way we pray and God responds, the fact that he can use us and our children as an analogy indicates there are similarities between our care of our children and God's care of us. This assumes that we **do** care for our children and that if we don't we are failing in our duty to them.

But for believers it implies more than this. It implies that our children will learn about God's loving care for them first of all through us. The whole idea of calling God by the name of 'Father' surely stresses this point. He is Father in the sense that he created us, that he begat us and that he goes on to care for those he has begotten. This is what we are to our children. They derived their life from us and depend on our care for their sustenance. As we give them this care they will learn how God cares, but in a much fuller way than we do, and without any of the hiccups that often mar our care of our children.

This is the first way in which our children begin to appear as 'special', for they begin to learn things that will eventually help them to know and trust God. Non-believers' children don't always have this. Some have positively bad parents who do not give them adequate care and may even ill-treat or abuse them. What can **they** possibly learn about God's fatherly care? How difficult it will be for them if they should come to be taught that God loves as a father! If God loves like my father, they may well think, I don't want him.

Others will give their children adequate care and genuine affection, but the children will not hear about God as Father from them, nor will they witness their father coming to God as his Father, in the way that **they** come to **him**. So they may never make the connection between their experience of their father and the character of God. However, if subsequently they do come to hear the gospel, it will be that much easier for them to get a right conception of God and respond to his invitation to come to him, than for children with bad fathers. They will also be able to look back and see that God's hand has been on them through childhood even though they weren't conscious of it. Augustine, although mischievous as a child and licentious as a youth, was able to trace God's hand drawing him to himself and to believe that God was as concerned for children as for adults. Even though his father might not have had a great deal to do with this conviction, his mother certainly did. Without going all the way with feminism and calling God 'Mother', we can certainly believe that God's care has a motherly as well as a fatherly character. He himself said through Isaiah, 'As a mother comforts her child so will I comfort you' (Isa. 66:13).

How good for us to know that even when we can't talk to our children about God because they can't understand, they can still be learning about him from our parental care, whether we are the father or mother! All this will be a vital preparation for the time when we shall be able to teach them in words. What we say will mean so much more if we have behaved towards them as God behaves towards us.

2. We are to avoid misleading them

As has already been established, children are born with a sinful nature, an in-built tendency to go astray from their earliest years. Nothing but divine regeneration can obviate this. The most fearsome punishments and mightiest judgements fail. The Great Flood is unique, yet even this left human nature where it was, so that God resolved not to repeat it: 'Never again will I curse the ground because of man, even though (or 'for') every inclination of his heart is evil from his childhood' (Gen. 8:21). These words God uttered after the Flood, when Noah and his family alone remained and all the ungodly had been drowned!

Moreover, children are ignorant of their true condition. They don't realise they have within them a powerful evil principle with the potential to lead them into all manner of wickedness. Nor do they understand that the world is an evil place bristling with temptations to commit all manner of sins. Least of all do they have a conception of a personal devil eager to exploit these weaknesses and secure his hold over the whole of their lives.

All this makes children particularly vulnerable. The first responsibility of parents, indeed of all adults, is to see we are not the cause of their falling into sin. The words of Jesus on this subject in Matthew 18:1-10 are quite devastating: 'if anyone causes one of these little ones who believe in me to sin, it would be better for him to have a large millstone hung around his neck and to be drowned in the depths of the sea' (v. 6). It is not certain that Jesus was only speaking of little children when he said 'who believe in me'. He may have been referring to all who have responded to his appeal of verses 3-4 and humbled themselves like a child in order to enter the kingdom — 'the babes' to whom he reveals the things of God as opposed to 'the wise and prudent' (Matt. 11:25).

Be that as it may he must have been speaking mainly of children in view of the context of his words. He had a child standing with him, who became a kind of visual aid to his remarks. His extreme language means it would be better to be drowned and put right out of sight of society than to lead a child into sin. This is similar to what he said of the one who would betray him: 'It would be better for him if he had not been born' (Matt. 26:24). The words which follow also recall his words about Judas: 'Woe to the world because of the things that cause people to sin! Such things must come, but woe to the man through whom they come' (v. 7). The severity of the judgement God inflicts on those who mislead children is similar to that which fell on Jesus' betrayer.

This led him to repeat some searching words first uttered in the Sermon on the Mount about the need for self-discipline: 'If your hand or your foot causes you to sin, cut it off and throw it away. It is better for you to enter life maimed or crippled than to have two hands or two feet and be thrown into eternal fire' (vs. 8-9, cf. Matt. 5:29-30). Any sacrifice we have to make to learn self-control is less painful than the consequences of misleading a child — both for the child and ourselves.

Paul used children's vulnerability as an analogy when he warned the Ephesians against false doctrine in Ephesians 4:14. Christ from his throne on high has bestowed gifts of ministry on his church to build up its members and make them mature. This is not only to conform them more to Christ but to fortify them against false teachers: 'Then we will no longer be infants, tossed back and forth by the waves and blown here and there by every wind of teaching and the cunning craftiness of men in their deceitful scheming.' Children are like sailing ships, blown this way and that by the influence of those who are cleverer and more powerful than they. They tend to follow the bad rather than the good example. David's life was a mixture of good and bad. His good example was followed by Solomon, his bad by Amnon, Absalom and Adonijah. It all shows how careful adults must be in their dealings with children.

In this connection parents have a particular responsibility. Christian parents whose children are special will want them not only to keep on the rails morally but to come to faith in Christ. They need to be careful about all they say and do which has any bearing, direct or indirect, upon their children. Paul warned parents in the congregation at Ephesus about this: 'Fathers, do not exasperate your children' (Eph. 6:4). Similarly he advised those at Colosse: 'Fathers, do not embitter your children or they will be discouraged' (Col. 3:21). This goes beyond misleading them and causing them to sin. It means creating in them a state of mind which renders them unreceptive to the parental training he goes on to speak about in the second part of Ephesians 6:4: 'bring them up in the training and instruction of the Lord'.

Parents who exasperate or embitter their children are not necessarily bad parents living dissolute lives. They may be the exact
opposite. They may lead blameless lives, scrupulous to a fault. But
they want their children to be exactly the same, and to begin now,
in their earliest years. They are so over-bearing, repressive and
particular that their children are deprived of all means of expressing
themselves, so that they become, as Paul says, 'discouraged' and
'embittered'. They rebel against this strict regime, break loose and
fall into those very sins the parents were bending over backwards to
keep them from. The strict control has become counter-productive.
They first fall into the sin of anger and resentment against their
parents, losing all respect for them; then grow up into more and more
sophisticated forms of sin.

There is a particular danger of this for some Christians at the
present time. The type of parent Paul has in mind is one we have
come to associate with the Victorian age; severe, stern, tyrannical.
Since the end of World War I there has been an increasing reaction
against that type of upbringing. It has been accompanied by a
slackening of the belief in human depravity in favour of the view that
human nature is essentially good. Children must not be repressed
but allowed to express themselves to the full. This has led to a
general breakdown in discipline — in society, school and home.
Many are alarmed at the consequences of this: juvenile delinquency
leading on to a general increase in crime; difficulties in educating
children at school, and parents' inability to control them.

Through fear of what may happen to their own children Christians are in danger of overreacting and returning to a Victorian
pattern. What is needed is to take our cue, not from what is
happening around us, but from the Bible. If we do so patiently and
calmly we shall be able to avoid, not only sending our children down
the road that many non-believers' children are travelling, but
actually hastening them down that road because of our exaggerated
approach.

For example, we can impose too may rules on them intending to
regulate their personal behaviour but only succeeding in making
them feel overrestricted. This applies particularly to what we expect
of them as regards religious activities. We ourselves have a routine
of daily devotions which we do not find irksome because we love the
Word of God and prayer. To miss them would be like going a day
without food. But just as our children have less on their plates at

meal times than we do because of the size of their stomachs, in the same way they can only take short periods of 'Family Prayers'. Similarly we enjoy a full round of Sunday services, with a sizeable chunk of devotional reading in the interval. But to expect the same of our children is to be in danger of what Paul called 'exasperating' them. At all costs we must avoid using our children to make a point to our ungodly neighbours, lest in the end our children are put off for life and furnish our ungodly neighbours with yet more ammunition against the gospel.

The same applies to the content of our teaching in the family. We can overemphasise sin, the law, and judgement in the hope of producing conviction of sin and the brokenness which opens the way for the gospel. But because we have read of this in our great biographies and sermons, and even experienced something of it ourselves, does not allow us automatically to impose it on our children. This kind of teaching is more appropriate for those with a more developed sense of moral and spiritual responsibility and greater sophistication. Our children do need to be made aware that they are outside the kingdom, but at the same time to see how well equipped they are while young to enter it. This calls for the gentle touch rather than the jack-boot.

If we do this we shall not only help our own children along, but be a witness to those parents who have imbibed the non-discipline approach of modern psychology, and show them that 'the opposite of wrong discipline is not absence of discipline but right discipline'. [27] This is exactly Paul's approach in Ephesians 6:4: 'Fathers, do not exasperate your children; **instead** bring them up in the training and instruction of the Lord.' The alternative to the over-bearing severity which only produces what it mistakenly sought to avoid is not to abandon discipline altogether, but to adopt the Lord's way of bringing up children. It remains for us to see what this is.

3. We are to educate them in the ways of God

'Bring them up', says Paul, that is, 'rear' or 'nurture' them. The term is used in secular literature of plants and animals as well as children. All need much care and attention lavished upon them if they are to realise their full potential. How much effort, time and money does the gardener bestow on his young plants, bushes and trees so that they might grow strong, beautiful and fruitful! The dog-lover acts similarly towards his animal in the hope that he will be able to exhibit it in the dog show. 'You are worth more than many sparrows', Jesus said (Matt. 10:29). He might have said we are worth more than flowers and trees, dogs and cats. He did say that one human soul is worth more than all the world (Mark 8:36-37). Therefore, if we are his disciples, the attention we give our children will far exceed anything we do for those lesser creatures we delight in. 'Sometimes one is given the impression that very little time and care, attention and thought are given to the rearing of children. That is one reason why the world is as it is today and why we are confronted by acute social problems at the present time. If people gave as much thought to the rearing of their children as they do to the rearing of animals and flowers, the situation would be very different'.[28] Dr Lloyd-Jones said these words nearly 35 years ago; how true they have proved.

The same word is used in Ephesians 5:29 and translated 'feed' in the N.I.V. It refers there to the care we lavish on our own bodies and which we should lavish on our marriage partners. All this is an illustration of the care Jesus has for his church because it is his body and bride. This is parallel to the passage in Matthew 7 quoted at the beginning of this chapter. We seek to treat our children as God treats us, not only because they deserve it, but because it teaches them, unconsciously at first, to know the kind of God he is. Gradually our children come to see what they mean to us and what we mean to God. So this is a very powerful educational tool. It is such considerations that make the family the ideal setting for the growth and development of children from babyhood to maturity. 'When God created man he made male and female, two in one; and he made them capable of giving birth to a third — the child; and indeed to several children — the family. Consequently it is in the context of a family that man is first born and reared, and later realises natural human completion and fulfilment in marriage and parenthood'.[29] This is not to say that the term 'family' may not be used where there is but one child, or even only one parent.

Paul was not speaking here of education and training in the contemporary sense — professional, technical and institutional. This has been discussed earlier. The type of education and training under consideration here is essentially domestic, carried out in the home where at least one of the parents is Christian. It is 'the training and instruction **of the Lord**'. This is entrusted to parents according to Scripture and should not be delegated to schools or other such institutions. Paul refers approvingly to Timothy: 'how from infancy you have known the Holy Scriptures, which are able to make you wise for salvation through faith in Christ Jesus' (2 Tim. 3:15). How successful this had been Paul observed earlier in the same letter: 'I have been reminded of your sincere faith, which first lived in your grandmother Lois and in your mother Eunice and I am persuaded now lives in you also' (1:5). This is what Paul meant by 'the training and instruction of the Lord'.

It is parallel to the famous words of Proverbs 22:6: 'Train a child in the way he should go, and when he is old he will not turn from it.' I understand the word translated 'train' originates from 'the palate or gums'. It was here that a rope was placed in the mouth of a young horse because it was a tender spot where he would feel every slight pull of the rope. In this manner he could be trained to go in the right way. I also understand that in Solomon's time it was the practice of midwives to massage a newborn baby's gums with date juice and thus trigger off its sucking sensation.[30] We could also compare it to growing trees. They must be staked to a straight post from the very beginning. Once they grow crooked it is virtually impossible to straighten them. The upbringing of a child in the ways of the Lord is very similar to these processes.

Paul refers to two aspects: 'training' or 'discipline' — the methods by which they are taught; and 'instruction' — the subjects which they are taught.

a. Training and discipline

The word used for 'training' — *paideia* (Greek) — is obviously derived from *pais* or *paidos*, 'child'. So 'training' means treating a child in a way appropriate to his condition. It corresponds to the word around which Proverbs revolves — *musar* (Hebrew). That book begins (after the Prologue) with the announcement or appeal, 'Listen, my son, to your father's instruction (*musar*) and do not forsake your mother's teaching (*Torah*)' (1:8). This does not imply a division of labour between the parents, suggesting that the father is responsible for the *musar* and the mother for the *Torah*. It is a Hebrew poetic way of saying both parents do both things. The two terms are very close to Paul's 'training and instruction'. In Proverbs this is done to bring the child out of his state of simplicity (1:4) and make him 'wise' and 'prudent' (1:2-3), so that he can live as a godly man in society.

In the fourth century A.D. John Chrysostom, Bishop of Constantinople, compared training children to fashioning a statue. 'Like the creators of statues, do you give all your leisure to fashioning these wonderful statues for God. And, as you remove what is superfluous and add what is lacking, inspect them day by day, to see what good qualities nature has supplied so that you will increase them, and what faults so that you will eradicate them'.[31] This reminds us that sculpting is a negative and positive occupation: some pieces have to be knocked off because they spoil the proportions; what remains needs shaping to conform it as closely as possible to the model. Training children is similar — it has its negative and positive aspects.

i. Positive training

Basically this means pointing the child in the right direction in the way a plant or tree is trained to grow straight upwards from the very start. Proverbs is still an excellent guide here, the most thorough in all Scripture. It needs to be translated from its old covenant mindset into that of the gospel, but once certain basic principles are grasped, this is not difficult. The old covenant offers to the obedient a long and prosperous life in the land God gave his people Israel; the new covenant blessing is eternal life in the Spirit enjoyed in the kingdom of God now and hereafter. Under the old covenant the way to blessing was obedience to the law, under the new it is faith in the obedience of Christ in his life and death. But the two are agreed on the concept of a whole life based on trust in and love for God, although the old uses the term 'fear' instead and speaks of godliness as 'wisdom'. 'The fear of the Lord is the beginning of wisdom' therefore means 'Trust in and love for God are the basis of true godliness and discipleship of Christ'.

The bulk of Proverbs contains details of how to live in society: how to think inwardly, how to speak to the like-minded and the hostile, how to get on with your neighbour, how to regard those in authority and benefit from their office, how to handle money and do business, how to make your farm prosper, how to have a happy domestic life, even how to choose a wife! The book probably originated from Solomon's recollections of his own upbringing by father David, which he compiled in order to educate his own vast family. Later it was edited together with other writings into a book for use in synagogues and homes. It is a pity it is not better known and used by God's people today.

ii. Negative training

Because of sin within and a wicked world without there will have to be negatives in a child's upbringing. There is a time for saying 'No' and 'Don't'. This takes various forms.

1. *Warnings.* In a fallen world dangers surround the growing child. The baby, as he begins to explore, has to be warned about the fire and the pussy-cat. The child as he begins to venture out on his own has to be made aware of the evils of society. This is what we find the father in Proverbs doing, especially in the early chapters before the Proverbs proper, which begin in chapter 10. There are bad youths and men out there wanting to recruit gullible lads into their gangs — Fagins looking for Olivers.[32] But women can be a danger too. There are those who for a price will try to lure the young man into their beds.[33] When we remember that those Solomon was warning his son against were Israelites, members of the 'holy nation' in covenant with God and under his law, how much more do we in our secular society need to warn our children!

2. *Prohibitions.* In some areas it is necessary to go beyond warning and lay down firm rules about what in any circumstances must not be done. We find an example of this in a later part of Proverbs which is not from the mouth of Solomon himself in 22:22—23:17, 20-22, 31. It is a string of 'don'ts': 'Do not exploit the poor', 'do not make friends with a hot-tempered man', 'do not strike hands in pledge', 'do not move an ancient boundary stone' and so on. One who has been trained to accept certain prohibitions in childhood will be prepared for these more adult ones.

3. *Punishment.* What if the warnings go unheeded and the rules are broken? If we are to follow God's dealings with **his** children in the way we treat ours, there will have to be a degree of punishment. Proverbs is well known for advocating punishment, because of its reference to 'the rod':

    13:24: 'he who spares the rod hates his son'.

    22:15: 'folly is bound up in the heart of a child, but the rod of discipline will drive it far from him'.

23:13f: 'Do not withhold discipline from a child; if you punish him with the rod he will not die. Punish him with the rod and save his soul from death'.

29:15: 'The rod of correction imparts wisdom, but a child left to himself disgraces his mother'.

Punishment can be retributive or remedial or a mixture of both. Ultimately retributive punishment is in the hands of God.[34] He has however to some extent delegated it to society through its magistrates.[35] While there may be an element of retribution in parental punishment, its main purpose will be to prevent the child from getting into the habit of wrong doing. This will then save it from society's severer punishments for more serious crimes.[36] A child disciplined at home is less likely than an undisciplined one to become a criminal who falls foul of the law.

The administering of punishment by a parent is not the easiest part of his role as a trainer. We who inflict it are ourselves not free from sin. This will affect the situation. Some parents are more conscious of this than others and feel, 'What right have I to inflict punishment?' Others are excessively tender and can scarcely bring themselves to inflict pain on their child. They may threaten but hold back from carrying out the threat. They fear they may lose the child's love if they cross or hurt him. If they do inflict punishment they will suffer emotionally far more and longer even than the child, and this will be an added disincentive. The effect may be the 'spoiling' which the old adage about 'sparing the rod' mentions.

Others are more choleric, unable to control the anger a naughty child arouses and will lay into it with little restraint. They will even derive some perverse satisfaction from making the child suffer. Both of these methods seem to be dictated more by human weakness than the need of the child. If the latter is our aim we shall approach the matter with consideration and method. We shall first have to realise that while our children are with us for much of the time every day they are going to irritate us frequently and break our rules regularly. We cannot inflict severe beatings for every offence without destroying our children and ourselves.

We can to some extent obviate this by using degrees of punishments. There is, for example, the **verbal** kind, the telling off. The severity of this can be on a sliding scale as regards the words chosen, the length of time taken, the tone of voice adopted and even the number of decibels attained! It needs to stop short of nagging, as John Inchley warns: 'Nagging always has the effect of belittling a child ... and can be so severe it amounts to mental cruelty'.[37] He refers us to the Living Bible's daring translation of Ephesians 6:4: 'Don't keep on nagging or scolding your children making them angry or resentful'. While this is not exactly what the apostle wrote, there is a good deal of truth in it.

Another form of punishment is to impose **additional rules** on them for a given period. God's law was imposed partly to restrain sin during the days of 'the church's' infancy, according to Paul in Galatians 3:24, where the marginal reading is preferable: 'until Christ came' is more accurate than 'to lead us to Christ' and more in keeping with the law's purpose. 'Until' the Redeemer came to save us from the reign of sin over us, it had to be restrained. This was the function of the law and its sanctions. Similarly, while children are young they need a number of clear and simple rules until they are able to think for and control themselves. So this would seem to be an almost divinely sanctioned form of punishment! Children cannot handle much freedom without abusing it. The best answer is to curtail it while they are learning how to use it.

What then of **corporal punishment**? To be effective rather than counter-productive it will need to be rare and restrained, and diminishing with the increasing maturity of the child. With the very young child the short sharp rap need inflict little pain, since its effectiveness lies in the shock rather than the hurt caused. Most parents practise this and it need not be a problem. Certain organisations in our society are trying to make it a problem and want it made illegal. This is because of the change in thinking from a Bible-based view to a secular one. Dr Lloyd-Jones preached at length on the disappearance of the whole notion of punishment in favour of a psychological approach.[38] Human nature is now seen as essentially good, so we are advised, 'What you must do is build up the goodness that is in the child and draw it out'.[39] This explains the modern revulsion against corporal and capital punishment. It has gone beyond a mere reaction against Victorian tyranny, since it is derived from a totally humanist world-view. Our danger is of reacting against this back to Victorianism. The said Doctor has some wise remarks about how to exercise discipline biblically without 'exasperating' our children. [40]

It is with the older child that the problem becomes most acute. When the mild slap becomes ineffective, do we resort to the stick?

If so, when? How many strokes? How heavily? No one can give definitive answers to these questions, about which we have to be persuaded in our own minds. We can't totally ignore the thinking of our society and send our children among their friends with bruises and weals on their anatomy for doing things their friends' parents would accept as normal. On the other hand we have the words of Proverbs nagging away at us and fear that if we 'spare the rod' we will 'spoil the child'.

But Proverbs does not mean that to beat our children is an absolute divine law which we are obliged to perform literally. It is not certain that we are even to take 'the rod' literally. References to it in such verses as 10:13, 14:3 and 22:8 are more likely to be metaphorical. God said he used 'the rod' on his erring people in Job 21:9, Isaiah 9:4 and Micah 6:9, meaning he temporarily removed his protection against their enemies, or their blessings of rain, food, etc. Similarly for us there are ways of making our children feel ashamed of their behaviour and changing it other than by hurting them physically. We can temporarily withdraw one or more of their pleasures, reduce their food intake without starving them or banish them from the family for an hour or two. As they mature they will become more sensitive to this treatment. Corporal punishment on the other hand is likely to hurt their dignity and self-respect and thus cause exasperation and bitterness against the inflicting parent, the very thing Paul is warning us to avoid. Proverbs 17:10 warns us that where 'folly' has become ingrained in the character no amount of corporal punishment will be effective.

This is a difficult area, necessitating thought, prayer, counsel and knowledge of our children's personalities, and our own too. But punishment will need to play some part in discipline and training. If it is well administered, far from creating resentment, it will be appreciated, because it will give a child a sense of security, teaching him where the boundaries of safe and acceptable behaviour lie. 'A child, even though he or she may be reluctant to admit it, also likes to be disciplined, and is much happier when an element of supervision is present, especially in his or her relationship with other children'.[41]

The best administered discipline, however, is not a cast-iron guarantee of producing a well-behaved child. God's punishment of the human race by the Flood failed to drive the endemic evil out of the hearts of young and old alike.[42] The words 'the rod of discipline will drive it (folly or sin) far from him' (Prov. 22:15) are not absolute. 'The rod' may fail, and we are in danger of thinking we haven't laid it on hard enough, so increasing it to alarming proportions without success. We may even produce a brute worse than ourselves. On the other hand, this must not make us give up altogether. We need to remember the other side — the danger of 'spoiling' by too indulgent an attitude, or blindly thinking they are so perfect they need no discipline. 'There are parents who think **too** highly of their own children. All their geese are swans. Other people's children are inferior. The result is their own sons and daughters grow up with an unattractive feeling of superiority and a false belief they are really more distinguished physically, intellectually or socially than their peers — until the moment of truth dawns and brutally shows otherwise'.[43]

b. Teaching and instruction

While 'training and discipline' are with a view to good behaviour 'teaching and instruction' are to impart knowledge and cultivate right thinking. As has been said more than once most Christians are not equipped to take total charge of the education of their children for living in a secular society in today's world. There are a few exceptionally able parents (often trained as teachers themselves in the State system!) who undertake this daunting task and do so successfully. Yet even they rely to an extent on material produced by professional educationists and put their children through public examinations. Many go on to further education provided by the State. Most of us do not go down that road, either because we feel incapable of doing justice to it or simply because we are not convinced about the theology behind it, which was discussed in an earlier section.

What we can and ought to do is what Paul refers to here, that is, impart to them 'the instruction of the Lord'. This simply means teaching them what the Scriptures say. We parents should do this because we have the best opportunity, having our children with us day after day for many years. Also this is something they are unlikely to receive at school, or if they do the presentation may well be unacceptable to us. The early church did not set up Bible education programmes for children, believing this to be the responsibility of parents. They did however write and preach to parents to help them discharge their responsibilities in this area.

William Barclay's researches into 'Educational Ideals in the Ancient World' led him to this conclusion: 'One thing becomes clear. The Church was far more concerned with the transmission of life than with the transmission of facts. The Church was not intensely concerned with schools as such; it was willing to use such schools as there were for the purposes of ordinary education. But the Church was intensely concerned with the home. The Church saw that in the last analysis the only true teachers of any child are the parents of that child ... The child is the gift of God to the parent, and the child must be the gift of the parent to God'.[44]

Children have a great capacity for learning, and for retaining what they learn in childhood. We have already considered what Proverbs says on the subject in 22:6. This has been proved true. Jerome in the fourth century wrote letters to his friends advising them how to bring up their children and emphasising the importance of their early training. He believed a child's early impressions were not easily erased. 'You cannot take the dye from wool that has been dyed,' he said. Most of us can remember things we heard and read as children far better than we can remember last Sunday's sermon. Parents who have children with them every day should take the utmost advantage of their opportunity to 'bring them up in the instruction of the Lord'. There are two aspects of the matter to consider: the subjects we teach and the methods we use.

i. The subjects we teach

What are the most important things for us to teach our children?

1. *The facts of Scripture.* First come the stories, the human events, which young children best relate to and which hold their interest. This is vital in any case because the teaching of the Bible arises from the events it relates. Christianity is historically based, it is about what happened, what God has done. The people of Israel sang songs about the mighty acts of God in their history.[45] Some of the greater events had special annual festivals to celebrate them. These formed the basis of what they taught their children,[46] who grew up with the clear knowledge that they belonged to a special nation. It had once been a slave people in Egypt, but God had brought it out, led it across the great Sinai desert, appeared personally to dictate its constitution,

then enabled them to fight their way into the land they now occupied and loved.

As the years went by more and more things happened which they had to keep in remembrance. Christian parents will acquaint their children with this Old Testament history rather sparingly at first, just giving the children enough to lead up to the story of the coming of Jesus, his life, death and resurrection and the subsequent acts of the apostles. Gradually the eternal truths will emerge from these stories, and they will begin to see God as Creator, Provider, Judge, Saviour and Lord, especially as he has revealed himself and acted in his Son. Thus from the stories will come the gospel itself.

2. *Obedience to parents*. For a child this is the first duty he needs to learn. Paul refers to the fifth commandment as 'the first commandment with promise'. Since there are no others with promises he must be saying two things here. One is that there is a sense in which the fifth commandment comes **first**, since it is the first thing we learn, even before we learn about God: 'the responsibility of children is primarily of obedience to their parents'.[47] The other is to point out that the commandment has a **promise** attached to it — for the Israelite it was the continuing tenure of the land of promise, and for the Christian membership of the kingdom of God.

As the stories of the Bible are taught so the children will become aware that many of these concern families like theirs, with mothers, fathers and children. Indeed at an early stage it is a good idea to concentrate on these rather than the bloodier episodes, not excluding the cross, which needs to be delayed until the reality of Jesus as a person has become clear by describing his works of healing and suchlike. In this way they will hear of good and bad parents, good and bad children, which form the basis on which to show why it is good and right to obey parents. It will also lead smoothly on to the next subject.

3. *Reverence for God*. Learning obedience to parents is a powerful incentive to cultivating reverence for God. The child learns to look up, to realise he hasn't the final say. As he develops he discovers others who have greater authority even than his parents, and who are also there for his protection and help: schoolteachers, police and government officials. It then becomes natural to take this a stage further and see there is One who is over those who are over him — God himself.

Along with this growing consciousness of a hierarchy in the world he will be hearing his parents and perhaps others praying to this God and singing to him. Where this is done with reverence and in a childlike spirit, the child will become aware of a God who is real if unseen. All this will build up a general atmosphere in the home by which Christ is a reality and plays a part in all the activities in the house: meals, work, news and general conversation. In the course of time he will connect all this with the God who appears in the stories and teachings of the Bible he is continually hearing about. Since 'the fear of (reverence for) the Lord is the beginning of wisdom (personal faith)' (Prov. 1:7) this aspect of the child's instruction is not the least important.

ii. The methods we use

The ways in which the instruction is carried out will need to develop as the child does. 'The relationship of children to parents is not static. It is dynamic and changing, for children grow from babyhood into boyhood or girlhood, and then on into their early teens when they are neither full-grown adults nor any longer children. Christian parents need to recognise the changing nature of their relationship with their children as they grow to maturity; otherwise they are likely to exasperate them'.[48]

1. *Answering their questions.* After a while telling stories and making statements will not be enough. Children will show their minds are developing by asking questions. Answering questions is one of the ways commended in ancient Israel for teaching them.[49] So we should not feel threatened if they question our statements, as if they were almost blaspheming. This is also a signal to us that they are ready to be asked questions and to be encouraged to think about what they are hearing or reading. This question-and-answer process also indicates they are acquiring to a limited extent the art of mental logic. We find this approach in the child Jesus in the only record we have of that phase of his life.[50] Gradually they will be able to think increasingly in abstract terms and begin to grasp some of the great truths about the invisible God. In these ways 'prudence is given to the simple and discretion to the young' (Prov. 1:4).

2. *Encouraging their response.* At all these stages we can look for some response to Jesus and God from the child and gently encourage it. They can be encouraged to use the Bible on their own, if necessary in an abbreviated, simplified and pictorial form. We can suggest they pray, preferably in their own words. Learning such prayers as the Lord's Prayer by heart and repeating it is not as good as naturally talking to God. What they actually say or ask matters very little at first provided they acquire the sense that he is there listening. Even if they pray 'Bless pussy' or 'Bless dolly' we need not stop to correct their theology at that stage!

Most of all we will be looking for a response to the call of the gospel to faith in Christ. Jesus wanted the young to 'come to him' (Matt. 19:14). As already observed, this is language they understand. They know what it means when mother or father say 'Come to me'. Encourage them to respond to Jesus like that — not necessarily in a once-for-all way, but as a response to whatever they hear of him. Let them come to him as they begin the day and as they end it. Let them come to him asking him to do for them whatever he offers, as found in his words and those of his apostles. There need not necessarily be one big 'come' which we chalk up as their 'conversion' and tell everyone about. Surely it's better to say 'I came to Jesus this morning' than to say 'I came to Jesus in 19—'. While John Inchley goes a bit far in using the word 'criminal' for the attitude which 'says this or that one is not a Christian because he has not conformed to some adult pattern of declared and conscious repentance and faith',[51] there is a good deal of truth in his observation.

Certainly we should not pressurise them into a 'decision'. But neither should we discourage them by telling them they aren't old enough or don't understand, otherwise we are in danger of the rebuke Jesus gave his disciples.[52] As they learn more of what 'sin' means and how they too are 'sinners', they will want to bring this burden to someone. When they learn that Jesus is the Saviour of sinners and that he did no less than die most cruelly to become their Saviour, they will want to 'come to him' with their sins and be saved from them. Then all our training and teaching will have proved fruitful and worthwhile.

Additional note:
It may not be stretching the term 'parental responsibility' too much to apply it to what we can **learn from** our children as well as to what

we **teach them**. Jesus made a childlike attitude essential to salvation.[53] Since becoming babes in mind makes us babes in Christ and children of God, this is an attitude which should mark our whole lives. As we grow in maturity and acquire greater knowledge of God and his ways we are apt to forget about childlikeness, especially when we ourselves have children under us to provide for and teach.

Yet if we can only see it, God has set before our eyes a continual example of what we should be like — in our own children. Let us see in their childhood some reflection of our spiritual childhood. Let us see in their **ignorance** our own — that we have hardly begun to know this infinite God and his ways. Let us see in their **docility**, their simple acceptance of what we tell them, the spirit we ourselves need to cultivate with our Father if we are to go on growing in knowledge. Let us see in their **sincerity**, their ingenuousness and freedom from hypocrisy and pretence, qualities immensely desirable for a Christian. As we see how quickly they grow out of this, and the 'deceitful heart' begins to make its presence felt, let us examine ourselves as to whether we have been 'led astray from our sincere and pure devotion to Christ' (2 Cor. 11:3). Let us see in their **trustful dependence** on us the purest aspect of a believer's relationship with the Father and seek to emulate it. The child is happy when those he trusts are present, however awful the circumstances and conditions; but in the most wonderful surroundings he is miserable if those he knows and trusts are absent. If we could learn to be like this with Christ we would know what it means to call him our 'shepherd'.

It was this perception that gave Jesus his high esteem of the child, very different from the attitude of both Jews and Gentiles in his time. 'Children, along with women, old men and slaves, were viewed as physically weak burdens on society who had little value for the wider life of the community. In Greece and Rome it was an accepted practice to abandon unwanted children along the road-sides to die'.[54]

Let this mind be in us that was in Jesus. But let us not go to the opposite extreme of which some are in danger at the present time of idolising them. Sin appears very early in these seeming little innocents and angels. Crying when they are in need soon becomes crying when they don't get their own way and can't control their young tempers. 'Even a child is known by his actions, by whether his conduct is pure and right' (Prov. 20:11). The qualities Jesus commended will not hide the manifestations of sin and the need for regeneration and faith. We need to achieve a balance between what we learn from them and what they need to learn from us. Then we shall have a truly blessed home and family life.

References

Section 3; Part A

1 See also 15:20; 23:15f, 24f; 28:7; 29:15,17
2 Gen. 15:2
3 Gen. 26:34f; 27:46
4 Gen. 34
5 Deut. 6:6-9, 20-23; Ps. 78, 145:4, Prov. 4:1-4
6 Exod. 20:5; Ezek. 18:2
7 *We and our children*, Ch. 3: 'The Covenant with believers and their children'
8 Rom. 1:30-32
9 Rom. 2:14f
10 Gen. 7:1,13; 1 Sam. 9:20; Amos 3:2
11 Ian Shaw: 'The Bible and the Family' in *Christian FamilyMatters* (Evangelical Press of Wales) p. 17
12 Gen. 15:18-22

Section 3; Part B

13 *All about Children*, p. 47
14 *Ibid.* pp. 46-47
15 *Ibid.* p. 47
16 *Ibid.* p. 49
17 Ezek. 36:25-27
18 'Children brought to Christ not to the Font'
19 See pp. 46-47; 76-77
20 Gen. 33:5; Deut. 28:4,11; Pss. 127, 128
21 E. Hulse: *Testimony of Baptism*, p. 114
22 Deut. 6:6-9; 11:18-21
23 C. H. Spurgeon: 'Children brought to Christ not to the Font'. See also the article on 'The Priority of Praying for our Children' based on the life of the Haldanes, in *Reformation Today*, No. 128, p. 17
24 R. Buckland: *Children and the Kingdom*, p. 47
25 John Inchley: *All about Children*, p. 44
26 E. Hulse: *Testimony of Baptism*, p. 80

Section 3; Part C

27 D. M. Lloyd-Jones: *Life in the Spirit* (Banner of Truth) p. 268
28 *Ibid.* p. 290
29 A. M. Stibbs: *Family Life Today* (Appleford: Marcham Manor Press) p. 17
30 *You and your Child* (author not known), p. 19
31 'The Right Way for Parents to bring up their Children'
32 Prov. 1:10-19
33 Prov. 7:6-23
34 Deut. 32:35; Rom. 12:19
35 Rom. 13:4
36 Deut. 21:18-21; Prov. 19:18
37 John Inchley: *Realities of Childhood*, p. 74
38 See Life in the Spirit, Sermon 19
39 *Ibid.* p. 267
40 *Ibid.* Sermon 20
41 John Inchley op. cit. p. 62
42 Gen. 8:21
43 *Ibid.* p. 75
44 Op. cit. p. 261
45 Pss. 78, 104, 105, 106, 107
46 Ps. 78:1-4
47 R. Buckland: *Children and the Kingdom*, p. 8
48 D. P. Kingdon in *Christian Family Matters* (Evangelical Press of Wales), p. 66. Ron Buckland summarises the four stages of development through which children pass during the first dozen or so years of their lives in *Children and God*, p. 72
49 Deut. 6:20-25; Jos. 4:21
50 Luke 2:46f
51 *All about Children*, p. 20
52 Mark 10:13-16
53 Matt. 11:25f; 18:3; John 3:3-5
54 Christian History Institute's *Glimpses* No. 31

Section IV:
Children and the church

All through our investigation into the Bible's theology of childhood we have been hampered by the lack of passages explicitly addressing our subject. Nowhere is this more so than in connection with the topic of children and the church.

We can at least be fairly certain that children were present in the congregations which the apostles founded. When Paul wrote to Colosse he addressed the children directly.[1] He did the same when he wrote to Ephesus.[2] These letters went to other churches too. The Colossian letter was to be sent to Laodicea and read there.[3] The Ephesian letter was probably a 'round robin', to be circulated among the churches of proconsular Asia. The words 'in Ephesus' in 1:1 do not appear in some early manuscripts, suggesting that the name of the destination was supplied as the letter was transported to each place. It was likely that children in places such as Smyrna, Thyatira, Philadelphia and others heard it read.

These passages have been thoroughly discussed already, since they really refer to the way children and parents relate to each other at home. But they have something to teach us about children and the church, since it would be in the congregation that both children and parents would first hear these words. It would appear that these apostolic letters were read out to the congregation to whom they were addressed when it assembled for worship.[3] There was no means of copying them and placing a copy in the hands of each family. So we can imagine a crowd gathered in a room in a large house or a lecture hall or other public building, or even the open air, listening to the public reading of a letter of Paul. The children no doubt struggled to keep their attention fixed while the early chapters unfolded the great mysteries of Christ and the gospel, but would prick up their ears when they heard the word 'Children!' Their concentration would be able to last for the short sentence or two which followed. Our task is to investigate the significance of the inclusion of children in these letters, rather than go deeply into the words themselves, which we have already done.

The context in which the words occur is of some relevance. In both Ephesians and Colossians the children are addressed along with wives and mothers, husbands and fathers, masters and slaves. It would appear that whole households were present, including slaves. There are references in the New Testament to whole households hearing the gospel, believing and being baptised, of which the two in Philippi are the best known and most detailed: that of Lydia[4] and that of the gaoler.[5] In the case of the former the household was probably mainly female, composed of Lydia's companions and servants, although male slaves may have been included. In the latter case, while children are not specified, there is no need to deny the possibility of their presence. This is of course an assumption, but it is also an assumption to say that it included parents, brothers and/or sisters of the gaoler. First-century households could be large and comprise several generations and various relationships. It was this type of family that would be present in the congregation at Colosse, Ephesus and other places where the letters were read.

Another interesting point is the context in which the appeal to children occurs. In Colossians it forms part of the general call to holiness and the particular duty of cultivating good relationships.[6] All members were to love each other, and surely that 'charity' would begin at home.

In the case of the Ephesian letter the whole passage addressed to members of the family[7] arises out of the call to mutual submission in 5:21: 'Submit to one another out of reverence to Christ'. The very grammar indicates the connection, for verse 22 lacks the word 'submit' and reads: 'Submit to one another ... wives to your husbands ...', showing that submission to each other in the church is first learned in the home. Elders learn how to manage churches by managing their families.[8] Members learn how to conduct themselves with their fellow-members by practising submission at home. In a church there are different kinds of people: male and female, older and younger. Each is to be treated in a way appropriate to his or her age and sex: wives to 'submit' to their husbands and the husbands to 'love' their wives. Children are to 'obey' their parents and fathers are not to 'exasperate' their children but 'bring them up' in the way of Christ. Slaves are to 'obey' their earthly masters, treating them with 'respect', and the masters are to treat their slaves 'in the same way', that is, with 'respect' for them, not only as human beings but as fellow Christians, remembering that Christ is 'both their master and yours'.

So while family relationships are important in themselves, they are also a microcosm of church life and therefore doubly important for the Christian. The way we get on with each other at home and at church are all of a piece. We should not be one thing at home and another in church. As far as children are concerned, by learning obedience at home they are not only 'pleasing the Lord' (Col. 3:20) but preparing themselves to be worthy members of the congregation they attend with their parents. This opens up the whole subject of children in the church.

A. CHILDREN AND THE MEMBERSHIP OF THE CHURCH

We have established that in the apostolic churches children attended the meetings along with their parents and others in the household. They even heard themselves addressed in the reading of the apostles' letters. But in what capacity were they there? Were they members? Can children be members? If so, how do we know if or when they are ready for membership? There are therefore two questions to address: their eligibility for membership and the way of identifying their readiness.

1. Eligibility

What is necessary for church membership? Whom should a church receive into its fellowship? The position of Paul appears to have been that the church should receive those whom Christ has received: 'Accept one another just as Christ has accepted you, in order to bring praise to God' (Rom. 15:7). That Christ does receive children has already been well established: 'Let the little children come to me and do not forbid them' (Matt. 19:14). 'Come to Christ' is a metaphorical way of saying 'believe in him' as the great invitation of Matthew 11:27-30 shows. To those who come to him as sinners and seekers ('weary and burdened') Jesus offers 'rest', or restoration of soul.[9] Those who respond are further invited to become his disciples: 'Take my yoke upon you and learn from me'. There seems no good reason for making a distinction between the 'come' of Matthew 11 and that of Matthew 19. Indeed, as has been said more than once, children are in some ways better suited for coming to Christ in the right spirit than adults, who have to 'become like little children' in order to be received by him.

Jesus in fact went further when he added that 'the kingdom of heaven belongs to such as they' (Matt. 19:14), that is, to those who come to him in a childlike spirit. What is Christ's 'kingdom'? It is not a territory, place or institution, but a spiritual concept — the reign of Christ, his king**ship**, his rule over all things. 'The kingdom' is where Christ is, where he rules, just as Satan's kingdom is where he holds sway. The two kingdoms clashed in the ministry of Jesus, especially where he exorcised the demons. When he did this he declared he was overthrowing Satan's kingdom and establishing his own: 'if I drive out demons by the Spirit of God then the kingdom of God has come upon you' (Matt. 12:28). According to Mark 9:14-27 children can be indwelt by demons; similarly they can be subjects of the kingdom of Christ.

While Jesus has 'all power in heaven and on earth' (Matt. 28:18) and even over the underworld (Phil. 2:10), his reign is most evident where it is acknowledged and gladly accepted, that is, among his people. At Caesarea Philippi, when the apostles confessed their faith in him, he immediately went on to speak of the kingdom[10] and even give a vision of it to three of them.[11] The apostles were to administer this kingdom in his name.[12] What that meant was that they were to go and plant churches in his name, then teach and organise them. So while the ideas of 'church' and 'kingdom' are not identical, we may regard the church as the chief expression of Christ's kingdom in the present age. In Ephesians 1:22 Paul says that Jesus was made 'head over all things for the church', which means that the principal way his kingdom operates is in his headship over the church.

Now Jesus said that believing children were in his kingdom, which means they are also in his church. Apparently Paul, when he wrote to the Colossians and Ephesians, regarded such children as in the church. This is evident from the spiritual language he uses in bidding them obey their parents. In Colossians 3:20 he says, 'this pleases the Lord'. He is assuming these children want to please the Lord, that they have responded to his invitation to come to him, that they are so thankful to know he died for them that they want to show it by 'pleasing him'. 'You want to please Christ?' Paul is asking, 'Well then the best thing you can do is to "obey your parents". That's the main thing Christ wants you to do while you're children.'

In Ephesians 6:1 he goes further: 'obey your parents in the Lord'. This is just how he addressed the grown-up members of the household: 'Wives, submit to your own husbands **as to the Lord** ... Husbands love your wives **just as Christ loved the church** ... Slaves, obey your earthly masters **just as you would obey Christ** ... Masters, treat your slaves **in the same way.**' We are all to treat each other in a way that is in keeping with our relationship with Christ — that is, in the way he treats us and them. So 'obey your parents in the Lord' means 'obey them as part of your relationship with him, out of love for him, in order to honour him'.

Such children are surely eligible to be regarded as members of the church, qualified to receive baptism and communion. Since their parents are also part of the church, there will be no question of dividing families as there would if the children of non-Christian families were involved. But the New Testament does not envisage this situation arising in connection with young children. We congratulate ourselves when we manage to gather children from non-Christian homes. Undoubtedly we are doing them a great service, but tensions arise at home if they become serious about Christ and the church. Apparently the apostolic church did not have these tensions because they did not employ this method. But this does not mean there are no problems to face or questions to ask in the matter. There is the acute question of how we can know when and if our children are in that condition that makes them eligible for membership, that they have 'come to Christ' and are 'in his kingdom' or 'in the Lord'.

2. Identification

Today we are familiar with the practice of identifying ourselves — producing our 'I.D.' as it is called — and thus proving we are who we claim to be. What 'I.D.' can a child give that he or she is qualified to be baptised, receive the Lord's Supper and be accepted into the church?

It does not appear that there is a special way for children to prove themselves that differs from the way adults show their eligibility. The qualification for these ordinances in the case of adults is voluntary open confession of personal faith in Christ, nothing more, nothing less. Some public acknowledgement of faith in Christ is essential or these ordinances will be as meaningless for children as they would be for adults.

However, in the case of children, there is a problem about eliciting this voluntary open confession. As was said in a previous chapter, it is easy to get children to **say** they are Christ's. Children are like people canvassed in opinion polls — the way the question is framed largely determines the answer that will be given. Children are particularly vulnerable to this if they are asked about their faith in Christ. They are keenly competitive and ambitious; it means much to them to give correct answers, be the question factual or spiritual. When asked a question, their subconscious mind is thinking, 'What answer can I give which will make him say "Right!"?' They have a dread of the word 'Wrong!' So if a Christian asks a child, 'Have you come to/trusted/given your heart and life to Jesus?' it is obvious to the child what answer the questioner wants to hear. Few children will say 'No!' To go ahead and baptise them with a view to welcoming them to the Lord's table and into membership on the strength of this response alone would be fatal. Where this is done it tends eventually to produce a largely nominal church membership, with disastrous results for future generations.

The best way is to adopt the same procedure as with adults: to make them clear about the terms of the gospel and leave them spontaneously to confess their faith in Christ. This does not necessarily mean we expect them to stand up in a meeting and give a testimony. That is not the only or necessarily the best way to confess Christ. It may emerge in other ways: conversations with parents or other Christians, or open prayer in the home or at a children's meeting. A child who is heard thanking Jesus for dying for his sins is giving one of the best proofs of faith that he can at his age. After all, is this not what the redeemed in heaven do continually?[13] This gives the opportunity to ask the child more directly about his relationship with Christ, for there is some prospect of more than a mere 'Yes' forthcoming. He can be asked, 'Will you tell me more about it?' If he does, this is a healthy sign of life and amounts to a 'voluntary open confession'.

In these circumstances what right has the church to withhold its ordinances from a child? The Ethiopian, after a conversation with Philip the evangelist, asked, 'Why shouldn't I be baptised?' (Acts 8:37). Philip could come up with no objection and baptised him. When Cornelius and his people responded to the gospel, Peter could only say, 'Can anyone keep these people from being baptised with water?' (Acts 10:47). No one raised any objection. Although these were not children in the natural sense, they had become children in the spiritual sense and are relevant to our question. Is there any valid objection why children who have voluntarily confessed Jesus in the same way should not be baptised and received into the church? Why should they be told, 'Wait until you are older'? Supposing they ask, 'How much older?' Who has the authority to fix an age? Does the Jewish Bar-mitzvah, by which a boy was made 'a son of the law' at age 13, help us, especially since Jesus probably underwent this ceremony?[14] Since this was compulsory and confined to males it clearly belongs to the law not the gospel. Under the gospel these acts are performed voluntarily and irrespective of age or sex.

Ron Buckland complains of the unreasonableness of many churches who withhold membership from children even though they encourage them to believe savingly in Christ. He quotes a Baptist report which draws attention to 'a false division between baptism and church membership' in the case of children: 'There are Baptists who readily baptise a young believer but will leave the question of church membership until later. Such a practice is neither scripturally nor theologically justifiable'. So, says Buckland, 'the child is left in limbo as a potential Christian. As in churches which practise infant baptism, he belongs but he doesn't belong'.[15]

In the case of children it appears we require more than faith; we require a maturity of understanding that brings the child up to the level of the adult. But if the essence of faith is childlike simplicity, why should we add to it? Should we not rather take more care over the adults and examine them for childlike simplicity, to see if they are partly trusting in their maturity and understanding or if they have truly 'changed and become like little children' (Matt. 18:3)?

Of course, there is no guarantee that a child's confession is genuine and will be lasting. But can the same not be said of the adult? Do they always fulfil their expectations? Yet we accept them gladly on trust. Why should we not do the same with children?

This is not to ignore the differences between adults and children and the problems these present. Their immaturity presents us with a difficulty as regards accepting them for baptism and membership. We cannot converse with them on an adult level. We find it difficult to get down to their level in questioning or interviewing them and they find it even more difficult to answer our questions. Another problem is the confused motives that may drive them to seek baptism. They may feel it puts them on an equal status with us, which may encourage precocity. On the other hand the pressures of their peers, especially their school-mates, may be a deterrent and hinder their profession of Christ.

Because of these problems some have felt it wiser not to entertain baptising children until their mid-teens. This may be the right course. On the other hand, accepting a child's profession doesn't involve baptising him next week. There is no reason why a longish preparation period should not precede baptism and membership. There must be some way of fulfilling these great gospel principles in the case of children. Perhaps we have just not faced up to how to accommodate believing children in our churches and need to do a great deal more positive thinking on it.

There are also problems about their attendance at the Lord's supper and Church meetings, but these can be looked at in the appropriate place. In any case, these problems must not be allowed to infringe the basic principle: that we receive whom Christ has received, old or young.

B. CHILDREN AND THE ELDERSHIP OF THE CHURCH

What is the relationship between the believing children of believing parents and the Pastor and elders of the church? We have very little data to provide us with an answer to this question. But we do have the passage which forms the basis of this whole section, indeed was the basis also of the section on the home. While it does not give explicit teaching on the subject, the fact that it is the only passage in which an apostle addresses children directly is instructive. From it we may deduce three things.

1. Elders encourage children to listen to their parents

When Paul addressed the children directly in Ephesians 6 and Colossians 3 he made no attempt to give what we would call 'a children's talk'. Not that this would have been out of place. His teaching in these two letters probably plumbs greater depths and reaches greater heights than in any other part of his correspondence. In Ephesians he set forth election, regeneration, the unity of the

church and its ministry, the principles of Christian behaviour and
mutual responsibility. In Colossians he delved into the mystery of
the person of Christ. What would the children present have understood of all this? The modern Pastor, conscious of this, might have
tried to say something simple and interesting, so that the children
would grasp the essence of it or at least feel he knew they were there
and did not want them to be bored. Perhaps we might have tried our
hand at 'A Child's Guide to the Doctrines of Grace'?

But the apostle does only one thing: he refers the children to their
parents. He makes no attempt to take over their 'training and
instruction' himself. That would be trespassing on the parents'
territory. So he confines himself to encouraging the children to
listen to their parents. We could deduce from this that the primary
responsibility of pastors and/or elders towards the children in their
congregation is to point them to the instruction of their parents rather
than to take it on themselves. They are under no obligation to set up
special meetings, classes or activities, or even give the children a
special slot in the services. Not that these things are wrong. Quite the
reverse; they can be of great help in a child's upbringing. It is good
for him to assemble with his peers, to be taught along with them, to
sing and pray together — and play too. But of this more will be said
later.

The point here is that this should not become a 'must' in church
life, rating alongside worship and preaching. When this happens it
is in danger of becoming a substitute for parental teaching. If the
church takes over the role of child-training, parents may abdicate it
to them. Elders and Pastors are not *in loco parentis* and need to be
careful they are not coming between parents and children in this
matter.

2. Elders encourage parents to teach their children

In directing children to listen to their parents Paul has by implication
laid an obligation on the parents. If the children are to listen to them,
the parents must have something to say to them. This obligation Paul
makes more explicit when he says, 'Fathers, do not exasperate your
children, but bring them up in the training and instruction of the
Lord' (Eph. 6:4). Such an assignment may well have exasperated
some of the fathers! How ever are they to do it? Not all were Jews
who had inherited the tradition of passing on the teachings of

Scripture from generation to generation. Many of them had emerged from paganism. The churches of Asia to which these letters were written contained some who had been worshippers of gods like Zeus (Jupiter) and Artemis (Diana). They themselves needed instruction; they were hardly fit to be instructors.

This is where the whole context of the letters is helpful. Paul is showing the grandeur of the redemption they had embraced when, under his preaching in synagogue or lecture hall, they had believed in Jesus. He is also showing them how this great scheme is being worked out in terms of personal behaviour and relationships. This is what **they** can now begin to do for their children — pass on to them the glories of the gospel in terms the children can receive. They who knew their children and were closest to them, who had them near every day for much of the day, were best fitted to teach them. Children have to be taught as they have to be fed — little by little, the food broken up into pieces small enough to swallow and digest. This is far better done in short sessions once or twice a day than in a long session once a week.

The general relevance of all this to our situation is fairly obvious. The Pastor and elders do all they can to help the parents to fulfil their obligation to 'bring up their children in the training and instruction of the Lord'. The best way is for the Pastor to teach the parents 'all the counsel of God', as Paul did in his churches (Acts 20:27). As the parents grow in understanding and feel the wonder of the doctrines of redemption, they will quickly acquire the ability to translate them into terms suitable for their children to accept. Special classes for parents on bringing up children are no doubt fine, but few pastors have the time or ability to conduct them. If they do, they can easily be distracted from the attention they pay to their pulpit ministry. But it is the latter that best prepares parents to instruct their children. As the Pastor opens up the whole Bible to them, and as God 'opens their minds so that they understand the Scriptures' (Luke 24:45), so they will be able to convey this to their children.

3. Elders impress on parents and children the importance of their children's redemption in the whole purpose of God

When Paul addressed the children in Ephesians 6, he backed up his appeal by quoting the fifth commandment. When originally issued this commandment was nothing less than the basis of Israel's tenure of the promised land: 'Honour your father and your mother, **so that you may live long in the land the Lord your God is giving you**' (Exod. 20:12). This does not mean 'so that you who are now children will live here to a ripe old age'. The 'you' refers to the nation as a whole down the generations. It specifies the way Israel as a nation may expect to occupy that land for the duration of the old covenant, and not be driven into exile for disobedience or neglecting God. It means that Israel's continuance in the land depended on her continuing obedience to the covenant. To ensure that this would happen successive generations must come to know its terms and observe them. This was why it was essential for children to be taught the terms of the covenant and to be directed to obey them. If they were to do this, they must listen to their parents, believe what they taught and obey the precepts. Then when they became parents the process would be repeated. As long as this went on, so long would they inhabit the land. It was when this system broke down that they were driven into exile.

But at the time Paul was writing the question of Israel's tenure of the land had become irrelevant. Messiah had come and set up a universal kingdom and church. The meek inherit the earth now! So Paul takes it on himself to alter the precise wording of a commandment! He is saying that what is at stake in this matter of child upbringing is even higher than what was at stake under the old covenant — no less than the continuance of the church on earth! If the kingdom of Christ is to go on from generation to generation, the gospel must be handed down from generation to generation. This was what Peter had preached at Pentecost: 'The promise is for you and your children and for all who are far off — for all whom the Lord our God will call' (Acts 2:39). As Israel handed the old covenant on down the generations, so must the church hand on the new covenant, the gospel. It does so chiefly, but not only, as believing parents instruct their children. Thank God he is able to bring people, both young and old, out of sheer paganism, but his normal way is to use believing parents. There is evidence that the spread of Christianity during the early centuries was achieved largely through the instruction of each rising generation.[16]

So one of the most essential things a Pastor can do for the children in his congregation is to impress on their parents just how vital it is that their children come to know and believe the gospel. It will not only save the children's own souls and unite the family in Christ, but it will ensure the gospel continues to be handed on to another generation, that the church will survive and that the kingdom of Christ will grow. Then who can tell how many more souls will be saved?

C. CHILDREN AND THE LIFE OF THE CHURCH

We are thinking of believing parents (or even a single believing parent) with a child or children whom they wish to share in the blessings they themselves have found in Christ. Much of this is done at home. But they will also want them to participate in the life of the church. They won't leave them behind when they set out for its services and activities. They will also want their children to profit from their attendance — more and more as they grow up. If this is to happen, the church in general needs to be aware of the presence of these children and find ways to cater for them, so that they will feel they are part of it from their youngest days until they are virtually adults.

Let us therefore look at the church from the child's point of view and see what kind of things are done or can be done so as to maximise their involvement.

1. The dedication of children

Believers who bear children after their own conversion and entrance into the church will probably consider whether to have their child dedicated in the church. We have spoken of how a parent will privately give a child back to God, as Hannah did with Samuel, praying that the child will come to know him at an early age and go on to serve and witness to him. The question here is, should there be a public ceremony of dedication in the local church?

There is no way we can know whether the children in the churches to which Paul wrote had been publicly dedicated. There is no reference to the practice in the whole New Testament. But that does not make it wrong. We do many things in our churches for which there is no specific biblical warrant but which we believe to be in the spirit of the Bible. Public dedication is the expression of something parents do in private which does have biblical warrant. Parents who privately dedicate their children do so in the hope that

God will accept them, make them his own and use them. Their worship, service and witness will be in and through the local church. There is no reason why this should not be recognised in a public dedication in that church. However, since it is not mentioned in the New Testament it is in no way an obligation and should not be regarded as such an invariable tradition that parents are expected to conform to it. It is entirely a voluntary decision on the part of the parents.

If it is done it needs to be clearly understood what it means and what it does not mean. It does not imply the child is already a Christian, nor does it make him a Christian. It is not the Baptists' substitute for infant baptism. It is not to give the parents the comfort of knowing that their children are safe 'if anything happens to them'. It is simply a public thanksgiving among friends that God has been gracious to them and in return they want God's gift to glorify him. God has brought a new life into the world, repeated his miracle of creation. He has given to a married couple a gift and a sign of his favour: 'sons are a heritage from the Lord, children a reward from him' (Ps. 127:3). He has given a child to parents who will bring to him or her the means of his saving grace: prayer, the word, worship and fellowship.

As well as thanking God they are welcoming the child into the world, saying he is wanted and needed and welcoming him into their particular family which wants and will love him. The other believers with whom they meet are also welcoming him among them, taking him to their hearts and undertaking to pray for and encourage both child and parents. Parents and friends alike are acknowledging that the survival of the church and its witness on earth depend on the handing on of the gospel to the next generation. When some of their number have children they see hope for the future and pledge themselves to do all they can to realise that hope by seeking the blessing of God on the family that is dedicating itself on that occasion.

From the child's point of view the dedication is a recognition that, as the child of a believer, it is 'special' or 'holy' in the sense described earlier. As he grows up, is told of his dedication and possibly sees other children dedicated, this will help convey to him a sense of his being 'special'.

2. Children's attendance

Parents need every encouragement to bring their children, however young, with them whenever possible. This will apply particularly to the Sunday worship services. The fact that some of the proceedings will be above the heads of the children is not a serious problem since it is a very temporary state of affairs. Even while they are unable to read at all or understand much of what is said there are still many advantages in their being present.

a. They will come into contact with other families

'It is not biblically inaccurate to see the church as a "family of families"', says Ron Buckland. 'Indeed, the more the local church can support its families in their problems and itself be an enlarged family, the greater the spiritual gain for the children concerned'.[17] This 'spiritual gain' is of course long term. It means the children will grow up realising there are other families like their own. They will mix with children who, like themselves, have mothers and fathers (or even just one parent) who believe and practise the things of God. Later they will find that most children and families are **unlike** their own. But if from their earliest days they are surrounded by families to whom they can relate this will help absorb the shock. Of course, not every one in the church will have or be part of a family. There will be elderly couples and single people of all ages, down to teenagers. As time goes by they will learn to relate to people of all kinds, not only to the mothers and fathers and their children.

Ron Buckland regards this as a greater benefit than a church which has 'its family experts who act as trouble-shooters and therapists. The church by use of its own Spirit-given gifts, however humble, can so act as to upbuild itself and its members through love. A basic reliance on expert knowledge "puffs up", but a basic reliance on practical love and concern "builds up", 1 Cor. 8:1'.[17]

A child growing up in this kind of atmosphere will be well protected against the social evils that are tearing so many families apart. There is a good hope that he will be able to set up his own stable family in due time. Also, as he grows up in this way, the whole church family will mature. His relationship with his own peers will have that deep bonding that brothers and sisters develop by being brought up together. He will also grow increasingly close to the older members. The generation gap will decrease and the church family be bound more closely together. What a strength that will be in the life of the church! How many problems will be avoided which often tear churches apart! It is not only that children benefit from their attendance; the whole church does so in the long term.

b. *They will learn to participate in acts of worship*

It is obvious there are problems in having young children in a congregation at worship. Their behaviour is likely to be erratic: calling out during the quietness of the prayer time, crying, pulling the hymn books to pieces, wandering around. Such things don't help the spirit of worship and particularly disturb the concentration of parents who seek to control them. Chastisement — verbal or corporal — may bring more disruption than the original misbehaviour; and the anger generated in the parents is hardly conducive to the joyful praise which should mark acts of worship. Because of this some parents will keep their children out of the congregation, or the church may organise crèches or separate activities for children.

Understandable and commendable though these efforts are, they are not the best answer to the problem. As Ron Buckland says, 'This simply reinforces the idea that worship is for adults only. It also creates congregations without children'.[18] It is better if parents can persevere and endure the hardship for a little while. Children pass through phases, but do so very quickly. But if the parents are to persevere they will need much support. The structure and conduct of the service will need to take account of the presence of children.

'Children bring their own gifts to worship. We need to make it more real, more understandable, more spontaneous, more informal, more immediate. The needs children bring to worship include:

*   to be acknowledged
*   to have preaching and prayers that relate to their lives, their hopes and fears
*   to sing hymns without complex metaphors
*   to be allowed attention which moves in and out of focus
*   to be directed into times of silence
*   to contribute appropriately from time to time
*   to see adults being both excited and honest about the Christian life'.[19]

Perhaps as important as all this, is the attitude of the other members. Some legally-minded Christians think it almost blasphemy if the voices or movements of children 'disturb' the solemnity of the service. They will become restless, scowl and even rebuke the parents concerned. This is counter-productive and, not to put too fine a point on it, ignorant. God's ways are not ours, and it is him we are supposed to be pleasing in our services. We should ask ourselves whether **he** minds these temporary and minor disturbances. The right way is for other members to sympathise with and encourage the parents to keep bringing their children. If they have had children of their own and have shared this experience in the past they should be able to give them some assurance that things will gradually improve.

An intolerant attitude will polarise the generations and do nothing to improve the children's behaviour. It will discourage the parents, may make them hesitate about bringing their children to the service at all, or even drive them into another church where their children are looked at more sympathetically. A more tolerant attitude on the part of the other members will relax the whole atmosphere, which in turn will enable the parent to control their children more calmly and maintain the spirit of worship in the service. It is all about the love which bears each others' burdens. Where it is in evidence there is far more likely to be true worship pleasing to Christ than where there is dead silence but tension between different kinds of members.

c. They will witness the special occasions of the church

What are the highlights of the church programme? The anniversaries: Church, Pastor, Sunday School, Ladies' meeting? Or the festivals: Christmas, Easter, Harvest? Useful and enjoyable though these may be, they are not what the church is about and we find little record of them either in the New Testament or the annals of church history. Surely the high points of church life are when someone comes to personal faith and is subsequently baptised. Quite likely the person will relate the experience to the church at the time of the baptism. In fact a number may do so on the same occasion. There will be unbelieving visitors present — relatives and friends of the candidates and others. The Pastor will give a simple proclamation of the gospel as it is depicted in baptism. Afterwards there will be joy expressed and love shown to the new converts by the members of the church. The presence of God is often felt more powerfully on such occasions than all the anniversaries and festivals put together.

If our children are there they will witness all this. Whether or not they consciously understand it all, it will have a powerful effect upon them. Children have been known after a baptism service to spend the next few days baptising their way through their entire collection of dolls in the bath or the back garden. Children's games are not trivial but very serious matters in which they act out the things that have struck them most deeply. How much joy it will give their parents to see them doing this, rather than running around shooting each other with imaginary tommy-guns, because they have seen it done on T.V.! On this point Erroll Hulse has written: 'Our children are not excluded from hearing the testimony of new converts, sometimes those of their own age. They observe the transformation of life in such new believers. Then all that is involved in conversion is portrayed in the actual ordinance. The involvement of the new believers in baptism and the joy of the local church are witnessed. The entrance of the converts into the enrichments and pleasures of the new covenant, joyful union with Father, Son and Holy Spirit, are likewise observed. The Holy Spirit sometimes uses the ordinance of believers' baptism, together with the witness wrapped up therein to convince the unconverted ones of the reality of faith, and of their own need to come to Christ in trustful obedience'.[20]

Then there is the question of the presence of children at the Lord's Supper and their participation. Ron Buckland ably argues for the latter, answering most of the objections commonly raised.[21] Many have muddied the waters on this subject by obscure arguments, but it is a basically simple matter. If a child is eligible for baptism and membership it is eligible for the Lord's supper. If we can find no reason for withholding the water of baptism, how can we find one for withholding the bread and wine of communion?

But in all probability the majority of our children who come to services with us will not have arrived at the position of having testified to personal faith in a way that indicates their readiness for baptism. What about their presence at the Lord's supper?

To look at it from the negative standpoint, why should they not be present at the Lord's supper as they are at other services, including baptism? Is the Lord's supper more holy than baptism? Is silence more necessary at it than at other services? Is it more incomprehensible to the young than baptism and other services?

In fact (to look at it more positively now), the reverse may be nearer the truth. Food and drink are the most common substances of life. Jesus deliberately chose to use them to represent his body and blood. Breaking the bread and pouring out the wine are clear and dramatic pictures of the breaking of his body and shedding of his blood on the cross. What better way of setting the cross before our children than this? Where children are present at the service it often commands their rapt attention. They forget to talk or even fidget! When the elements are served and their parents and others physically eat and drink, their curiosity is aroused and they may even be awed. What happened at the Passover soon happens at the Lord's supper: they ask, 'What does this mean?' (Exod. 13:14). Just as the Israelite parents were able to use this as an opportunity to get them to listen to the story of how God brought them out of Egypt, so Christian parents have a great opportunity to tell their children of Jesus coming to rescue his people from sin, Satan and judgement.

If children are to be present at the Lord's supper it may mean some rearrangement of the service and perhaps the church programme. There will need to be at least one occasion periodically when the Lord's supper is not separated from a normal worship service but included in the one where most families are present. Nor will it take place after the conclusion of such a service when the children will already have sat a long time and families are thinking of going home. It is best at the beginning of a normal morning service. It will be a good discipline for the minister to keep it simple and brief, which is how it is best conducted anyway. If this is done occasionally, not more than once a month, and possibly less, it will retain its 'specialness' for the young, and the older too.

Surely it is best to build the church programme around services the Lord ordained rather than around those he didn't?

3. Children's meetings

Sunday Schools originated to meet a social rather than spiritual need. The Industrial Revolution brought families into towns and cities. All, apart from the very youngest children, went to work in the factories. Children received no education and were growing up illiterate, unprincipled and undisciplined. Although the phrase had not then been coined, it was an age of 'juvenile delinquency'. Robert Raikes was not the first to hold Sunday Schools but he was certainly a pioneer in the movement. His idea was to use Sunday, because it was the only non-working day for most children, to educate them, mainly in literacy. His programme included some attendance at church for catechising, but this took place after several hours' general education.

As the State gradually restricted the employment of children in factories and began to set up schools for them, so the character of Sunday Schools changed. Children who attended school all week and received their basic education there began to come to Sunday School for religious instruction. It is Sunday School in this sense that we have inherited and which we need to investigate. If the term 'School' is retained, which is questionable, it must certainly convey something different from its former connotation.

The first thing to clarify is what and whom we are aiming at. Since our book is written for 'believers and **their** children', it is at them we are aiming. We have to give weight to this since the general evangelical concept of a Sunday School is as an evangelistic agency for children from non-Christian families. The need for and importance of such an agency can hardly be overstressed.

We live in an age of **ignorance** of the basic facts of Christianity. There is no time like childhood for acquainting our generation with the truth of the gospel. They need a clear, simple, factual, interesting, lively, realistic presentation of what the Bible is about. We live in an age of **confusion**, when what passes for Christianity in society, including the media and the education system, is wide of the mark. The children need help in distinguishing the wheat from the chaff. 'Today much of the challenge revolves around demythologising the education that a child typically receives in our culture, and providing a biblical basis to counteract it'.[22] We live in an age when the current **world-view** is further away from the Bible's world-view than it has been since the days before Christianity first took root in our islands. For although the medieval church was unevangelical, and although there have been periods of decline since the Reformation until this century, there were always residual generally accepted assumptions about the existence of God, the earthly life of Jesus Christ, the need for personal and social morality, which have now been discarded by the majority, or at least by those who call the tunes.

The rising generation of children therefore needs us to 'rescue them from the foul rape of the mind carried out by this present world'.[23] In other words, Sunday Schools have a vital place, not only in saving individual souls from sin and hell, and in delivering the church from extinction, but in rescuing society itself from itself — a catastrophe which always overtakes people who become totally materialistic and secular. Instruction in the Bible will do more than any other single factor to obviate this situation. But we have to remember that the children who come to us without their parents are not our children. We should refrain from too much moralising, spiritualising and calling for decisions, which may create difficulties for the children at home and even divide the families from which they come. Our best service to them will be to acquaint them with the facts, especially of the life of Jesus, who he was, what he did and the meaning of these facts. Mr Gradgrind has had a bad press for his adulation of 'facts' as the be-all and end-all of education. But we can't do without them, nor can Christianity survive without a knowledge of them.

Thank God our children are not in the position of those we have just described, or at least only partially so. They do indeed confront and are confronted by 'this present evil age' (Gal. 1:4). They go to the same schools as the others (most of them!) and are thus exposed to the ideas and lifestyles of the present generation of teachers. They mix with children of their own age from unbelieving families and imbibe some of their values. They watch the T.V. and read the literature put out by the worldly-minded people of our times. They breathe much of the atmosphere that is foreign to that which they breathe in their families and churches.

But all this is to a great extent controlled and counteracted by the home and church influences about which we have written at length. Christian parents have their children under their wings for several years before they start to fly the nest for a few hours a day. The ground can be so prepared that it will largely reject the bad seed which is being scattered in their direction. For the next dozen or so years the influence of parents predominates over all others and can see them through the troubled times they will experience. They may not emerge unscathed, but they will emerge! As regards knowledge of the Bible, the gospel and Christianity the situation is a lot happier. If parents fulfil the role given them in, for example, Ephesians 6:1-4 their children will know the facts and even be able to distinguish truth from error.

This brief description of the children of non-Christian and Christian parents should convince us of the world of difference there is between them. Yet the general practice of evangelical churches is to put all the children together indiscriminately. The result is that the Christians' children hear what they already know well, and are in danger of becoming puffed up by their superiority to their friends who are ignorant through no fault of their own. The alternative scenario is that all are taught at the level of the Christians' children, with the result that the outsiders are totally out of their depth. There is also a danger that the Christian parents will unconsciously regard their children as in a similar position to those of non-Christians, and will leave their biblical education in the hands of Sunday School teachers. They may even be Sunday School teachers themselves, with their own children in their classes, and feel there is no point in repeating their Sunday School lessons at home!

There is surely a case, if the church is to have Sunday Schools or special children's meetings under some other name, for segregating the Christians' children from others. Some might argue that, since they are taught by their parents at home and attend church services, they need no special meetings. The point was made earlier that the instruction of children is the responsibility of parents and the eldership should not interfere. No doubt elders and parents can agree together as to how the former can help the children without trespassing on the parents' territory. For there are distinct advantages in having meetings for the children of Christian parents. Children enjoy being with their peers and we should not deny them enjoyment except where it is harmful. The sense of equality will be good for their confidence. On the one hand they won't feel **inferior** as at home and in church; on the other they won't feel **superior** as in the open Sunday School. As they grow up together friendships will be formed which may last a lifetime, in some cases leading to good marriages.

In a children's meeting they will feel more free than in an adult service and be able to begin to express themselves on spiritual subjects. They can be encouraged to participate in prayer and singing. Above all they can be taught at their own level. What their parents have already given them can be built upon. They can learn to discuss the lesson and how to relate it to their lives as children.

They can thus be built up and even help to build each other up, all good preparation for adult membership. They can have recreational activities and outings, depending on the availability of church members to staff them.

Not all will see things in this way. There are obviously logistical problems in holding two types of children's meeting at the same time, when many churches are overstretched in staffing one! There is also a case for saying that having believers' children and 'outsiders' together is of mutual benefit. It shows that the same basic needs are in all children irrespective. It makes the believers' children aware of those who are less favoured than themselves and more thankful for their 'Christian homes'. It challenges the outsiders' children when they discover that children of their own age can be enthusiastic about the Bible and the Lord.

No one can lay down a blueprint for children's ministry in all churches. However, it may be time we reviewed our approach and at least considered the benefits of segregation. Our great aim needs to be to use all possible ways to make our children feel 'special' and thereby encourage them to come to faith.

Whatever method is adopted it is important that children's meetings should not impinge upon the general worship and fellowship of the congregation. At all costs we should avoid bifurcating into two churches. Where the children's meeting runs parallel with the worship service it not only involves removing the children but several of the members as well. Some way needs to be found of giving the children their own activity without cutting the congregation into pieces.

In an area in which the New Testament gives us no specific guidance, it is impossible (indeed it would be wrong) to lay down specific patterns of how particular churches cater for the children among them. Much will depend on the traditions handed down, the current methods being employed, the numbers of children present, whether they are mainly members' children or 'outsiders', the facilities available and so on.

Some churches may feel they can keep the children in the same room as the adults for the whole time of the service by giving them some activity to work on during a part of the service. This will apply especially to churches which hold their children's classes before the main service or at some other time. Others will have a period of combined 'all-age' worship, then break up into groups so that the younger are taught at their own level. While this option has much going for it, it has the disadvantage of depriving the teachers of their own instruction, which, if they are to teach others, they need themselves. It is for each church to find the best way of implementing these principles so that they fulfil their responsibility to the children God has given them.

This in fact raises the whole question of the part of children in the adult activities of the church. The possibility of some children being baptised and becoming church members at an early age has already been discussed. But once they become members what part will they play in the adult life of the church, since most other members will be adults?

4 Children and adult meetings

The part children play in the membership of the church has to be related to their nature as children. They may be believers, baptised, communicants and members, but they are still children. We can only expect of them what we expect of any children while they are children. As children they are mentally and physically undeveloped and it would be inappropriate to impose on them all the obligations required of adult members. Bible studies, prayer meetings and church business meetings which require maturity are unsuitable for children. In fact where they continue until late in the evening they are beyond the physical capacity of children until they are well into their teens.

In addition to this they are subject to the authority of their parents and not directly under pastors or elders. It is for parents not pastors to determine a child's routine. A wise parent will see that a child who has worked all day at school has some mental relaxation and physical stimulation rather than lengthy meetings. He will also know that the child needs plenty of sleep. For these reasons a child's participation in the life of the church will be limited during its childhood.

But this is no reason why they should not be welcome to participate in those activities which suit them. They will already be attending Sunday services and possibly a special children's meeting. There may also be a recreational time during the week or at weekends. If they are not already overstretched an occasional meeting for 'junior members' could be arranged, corresponding to the adult members' 'Church meeting'. At this they can slowly be introduced to the full life of the church and instructed in the meaning of membership. No doubt they will have had a series of classes prior to baptism and reception into membership. This could lead on to a course in 'discipleship' until they gradually become absorbed into the full life of the church.

Then they 'will no longer be infants, tossed back and forth by the waves, and blown here and there by every wind of teaching and by the cunning craftiness of men in their deceitful scheming. Instead, speaking the truth in love, (they) will in all things grow up into him who is the Head, that is, Christ. From him the whole body, joined and held together by every supporting ligament, grows and builds itself up in love, as each part does its work' (Eph. 4:14-16). So this whole matter of 'believers and their children' is not just about how we best handle a temporary period in their and our lives, but about how we build the church itself. The benefits to our churches of handling childhood rightly are incalculable. It is so worthwhile taking it seriously and treating it as a long-term exercise.

References

Section IV

1   Col. 3:20
2   Eph. 6:1-3
3   Col. 4:16
4   Acts 16:13-15
5   Acts 16:29-34
6   Col. 3:12-14
7   Eph. 5:22 — 6:9
8   1 Tim. 3:4-5
9   cf. Ps. 23:3
10 Matt. 16:15-18
11 Matt. 16:28 — 17:5
12 Matt. 16:19
13 Rev. 5:9-14
14 Luke 2:42
15 Ron Buckland: *Children of God,* p. 94
16 See Terence Aldridge: 'The Spiritual Nurture of Children' in *The Ideal Church* (Carey Conference Papers, 1972).
17 *Children and the Kingdom,* p. 47
18 *Children and God,* p. 101
19 *Ibid,* p. 103
20 *Testimony of Baptism,* p. 80
21 *Children and God,* ch. 7
22 Christian History Institute *Glimpses* Notes to Issue 34
23 Peter Masters in *Sword and Trowel* 1992 No:2, p. 4

Epilogue:
The glory of the family

'By wisdom a house is built, and through understanding it is established; through knowledge its rooms are filled with rare and beautiful treasures' (Prov. 24:3f).

Scripture often uses the word 'house' to refer to its inhabitants — the 'household' or 'family'. It speaks of 'the house of David' meaning all his descendants. Psalm 127, which has been alluded to more than once in these pages, begins with the words 'Unless the Lord builds the house, its builders labour in vain', then goes on to speak of the various members of the family. Jesus spoke of a 'house(hold) divided against itself' (Matt. 12:25). Nowhere are the similarities between house and family better seen than in this proverb.

1.   Like a house a family has to be 'built'

People haven't always lived in houses. For long periods they dwelt in caves, trees and holes in the ground. Then someone thought of taking the materials from the cave, the tree and the ground and making them into a house. Whoever did this was certainly endued with great '**wisdom**', for so much more can be done with a house than with these more primitive habitats. It can have doors, windows, floors, rooms and chimneys. It can accommodate more people and possessions. There is almost no limit to its size.

The idea of the family too was the fruit of 'wisdom', but it was God's wisdom. He thought to make us in such a way that none of us is totally adequate on our own. Man and woman need each other. They need children and the children need them. The family has advantages over the loner:

'Two are better than one, because they have a good return for their work. If one falls down his friend can help him. But pity the man who falls and has no one to help him up! Also, if two lie down together they will keep warm. But how can one keep warm alone? Though one may be overpowered, two can defend themselves. A cord of three strands is not quickly broken' (Eccles. 4:9-12).

The anti-family spirit that has crept into our society is foolish for, although it has its drawbacks, the family has been proved the best method of living in the world. We shall have to get back to it eventually. Even the secular State recognises this; where it finds lone children it tends to place them with families.

We who believe that God's 'wisdom' is revealed in the Bible rejoice in its teaching on the family which we have looked at in this little volume, and want to do all we can to practise it. We will want God to 'build our house' and so will seek to do everything according to his word — obeying its precepts and trusting its promises.

2. Like a house a family has to be 'established'

The plans of a building have to be drawn up, the materials assembled and then, hardest of all, fitted together in such a way that they serve their purpose and stand up to the elements.

The easy part of family life is getting married and having children. The harder part is getting on happily together and enjoying each other's company. This isn't automatic; it has to be worked at. Where it doesn't come about, instead of being the greatest happiness, the family is the greatest misery — we are better off on our own, as Solomon pointed out more than once in his Book of Proverbs. The problem may be between husband and wife (21:9, 19; 25:24; 27:15), or between parents and children (10:1; 15:20; 17:21; 19:13; 29:3). My readers don't need convincing that in our contemporary society this is true in a big way. What is the cause? Even more important, what is the remedy?

Solomon puts it in one word — **'understanding'**. We don't make the effort to understand each other. Perhaps we don't even see the need. We come into marriage with an image of what our partner should be. We decide what we want our children to be like, even sometimes what career we want them to follow, although this is not as common as it used to be. We forget the basic principle of God's creation — diversity, variety. No two snowflakes are alike. All our fingerprints are different. So are our personalities.

154   *Special children?*

What we need to do is to 'understand' each other, how the other person differs from us, and to accept each other for what we are. For though this may not be what we want, it is what God wants. If we try to mould another person, even a young child, to our preconceived pattern, we shall be working against God and heading for disaster, however much we may be convinced we are right and are praying for that one. The friction involved in the process of trying to change each other is what often breaks families up.

We could apply this to the church, God's 'household' or family. Churches fall apart for exactly the same reason as families — we want everyone else to be just like us. But the church is a 'body' with all its variety, yet in which each part has a contribution to make to the whole. If we will 'understand' this and apply it to our estimate of our fellow-Christians our churches will be a lot happier.

3. Like a building a family needs to be 'filled'

The development and improvement of the house through history is an interesting study. At first there was just one room, then gradually came rooms allocated to different functions: cooking, eating, washing, resting, sleeping, playing, working. These activities required equipment, so came furniture and utensils. All this grew as '**knowledge**' grew — knowledge of the family's needs and how they could be met.

In the same way a family needs 'knowledge' of its potential. Each member has particular talents which determine the role he or she plays. The man brings his strength and skill, the woman her domesticity. Even the children have a contribution to make as their knowledge and talents develop. The time may even come when they take over from the parents.

The great thing is to share all this. The division of the house into rooms was not to give members of the family scope for leading separate lives, for these were shared. Everything brought into the house enriched it for everyone. In the same way each needs to know what the functions and abilities of all members of the family are in order that they might share the benefit of them together. Then the family will not merely be 'established' and stay together, but really enjoy doing so. Their home, their family and personal lives will be 'filled' with the riches of shared love and service.

4. Like a house a family needs 'beautiful treasures'

This was the final stage in the development of the house: to make it beautiful as well as functional. The stone was carved, the wood painted, the walls papered, the ceilings plastered. Furniture was designed. Pictures and ornaments collected and placed round the house. Who of us doesn't delight to visit those opulent mansions that our forbears set up in the eighteenth and nineteenth centuries? We even try to make our own humble abodes resemble them in a small way. We can't afford the originals, but we can have our reproduction Constables and Chippendales.

While the Bible-believing family will rightly delight in these 'beautiful treasures' and thank God for them, they won't be enough. They will look for other adornments. It is not only women who should 'adorn themselves with good deeds' (1 Tim. 2:9f) and 'a gentle and quiet spirit' (1 Peter 3:4). All of us are to behave in such a way, particularly in our personal relationships, that we 'will make the teaching about God our Saviour attractive' (Titus 2:10).

There is no question that a family which fulfils God's purpose for that institution is one of the most beautiful things on earth. Where it is 'the Lord' who 'builds the house', it will be a strong witness to the gospel. It will back up the public preaching and personal testimony in a unique way. It will be a healthy influence in the church fellowship, the neighbourhood and society at large. Let us be encouraged to work out and practise the teachings of Scripture we have investigated in this book. We shall be doing more for the cause and kingdom of Christ than we may realise.

Index of Subjects

Index of Scriptures